Counsel for the Accused Marine Corps Drill Sergeant

Counsel for the Accused Marine Corps Drill Sergeant

—

Marie Costello-Inserra

ISBN: 0692595244
ISBN 13: 9780692595244
Library of Congress Control Number: 2015920650
Marie Costello Inserra, Cary, NC

For my parents,
Tom and Anne Costello

Acknowledgements

———

I WISH TO ACKNOWLEDGE MY family and friends who offered support and valuable input in the writing of this book. To my husband, Paul Inserra, for unwavering faith, love and constructive criticism. To my friends, Joe McGowan for his insight, Anne Tabacco and Geri Nettles for their encouragement, Kenya Allen for helping me find the voice of the book. To Glory Paglini, Marion Inserra, Rich and Peg Inserra for reading the early drafts, and to Jodi Salamino for initiating the dialogue that started this work.

Abbreviations and military titles follow the Chicago Manual of Style.

A portion of the proceeds from this book will go to support our alma mater, Fordham University School of Law and to the Chesty Puller House.

Contents

Introduction

———

ON THE MORNING OF AUGUST 3, 1956, in a Parris Island auditorium that was designated as the temporary courtroom for the court-martial of United States Marine Corps S. Sgt. Matthew McKeon, Emile Zola Berman, counsel for the accused, rose from his seat next to Sergeant McKeon to offer his closing argument. It was hot—South Carolina summer hot. The school-auditorium-turned-courtroom was filled with reporters who had covered this story of tragedy, death, retribution, and remorse. It was a news story that ran nationally in every newspaper, every day since April 8, 1956, the day Sergeant McKeon took his platoon of seventy-eight men for a night exercise in Ribbon Creek, Parris Island. Only seventy-two returned; six Marine recruits drowned during the exercise.

My mother, Anne McKeon Costello, sat close behind her brother, Sergeant McKeon, watching the defense table where Thomas Costello, her husband and my father, sat with Berman as part of the defense counsel team of lawyers defending Sergeant McKeon. In the first row of the overfilled auditorium, my mother was joined by Sergeant McKeon's wife, Betty, who was seven months pregnant at the time, and his brothers, James McKeon and Edward McKeon. Both brothers were retired Marines and veterans of World War II, and both my parents were army veterans of World War II. My father was a private, and my mother served as a United States Army nurse. The youngest of the McKeon family of eight, Francis, also joined them in the crowded room awaiting the closing remarks of Sergeant McKeon's counsel.

Sergeant McKeon's lead counsel, Emile Zola Berman, was a slight man with an oversize gift to beguile a courtroom. His presentations in courtrooms clarified the facts and law of a case through his acumen of the human heart. Wire-rim spectacles framed his narrow face and rested on a long prominent nose. His impeccably tailored suits were from New York City, the city that gave him his law degree from New York University Law School in 1924. In return, he had given thirty years at the New York Bar before that morning of his closing argument in 1956 in the general court-martial of S. Sgt. Matthew C. McKeon, 668581, United States Marine Corps, Third Recruit Training Battalion, Marine Corps Recruit Depot, Parris Island, South Carolina.

Seated next to Berman was Sergeant McKeon. Sergeant McKeon sat straight and tall in the wooden chair at the counsel table that had been his for the past three weeks of his court-martial on manslaughter charges, alleged oppression of troops, and culpable negligence. Sergeant McKeon's face was drawn, with high cheekbones and blue eyes that looked ahead in the steady and clear vision of the experienced yet war-weary veteran of two wars that he was. Sergeant McKeon's spine barely brushed the back of the chair as he sat in attention for the entire time he was on trial.

The seats at the counsel table were filled with several civilian and Judge Advocate General's Corps, the legal branch of the military concerned with military law, who had worked with the lead defense counselor, Berman. Berman and my father were both admitted to practice law in the State of New York and had both left their practices in New York to work on Sergeant McKeon's defense. My father was there for family. Berman was there by the fate of his name and by his dedication to the law itself. For Berman, the law was an unquenchable promise for justice that he kept every day in the courtrooms privileged to hear him.

The prosecution—or as referred to in the trial record and in court-martial vernacular, the trial counsel—was sitting across from the defense table. Major Sevier of the Marine Corps prosecution team had just finished a closing argument that began with a recitation of the four charges and five specifications against Sergeant McKeon. The charges were as follows:

- Charge one, a violation of Uniform Code of Military Justice Article 92, alleged a breach of an order that prohibited alcohol on base.
- Charge two, oppression of troops, alleged a violation of Article 93.
- Charge three alleged two specifications of involuntary manslaughter in violation of Article 119 of the Code.
- Charge four, a violation of the General Article 134, alleged that the accused did wrongfully drink intoxicants in front of a recruit.

A jury comprised of six Marine Corps officers and one naval doctor was convened by the secretary of the navy to decide whether the death of six Marine recruits was a tragic accident caused by panic or whether it was manslaughter caused by criminal behavior.

When Berman stood to start his closing argument, four months of legal work by his team of lawyers rose up with him. The backstory of the lawyer's craft was woven into his words via the barely discernable sound of research, writing, submission of briefs and memos of law, investigation, interviews with witnesses, travel, review of expert reports, outline of direct and cross-examinations, preparation of exhibits, document review, preparation of digests of past testimony and statements, and the finely discreet art of strategizing the presentation of evidence in the battlefield of persuasion. Although this work is the same work of every well-prepared trial lawyer, what was different in this case was that Berman and the team of lawyers working with him were all working pro bono, more commonly referred to as working for free.

The jury of seven officers were chosen by Secretary of the Navy Charles S. Thomas. They were Col. Edward Huctinson, Lt. Col. Nicholas August Sisak, Lt. Col. Duane Fultz, Lt. Col. Daniel Joseph Regan, Maj. Edwin

Thomas Carlton, Maj. John Gust Demas, and Lt. (Medical Corps) Bentley A. Nelson. Irving Klein served as the law officer, or judge. The gravamen of the issue that these men were called upon to decide was the cause of the drownings that occurred during the exercise. In short, was it an accident, or was it caused by the criminally culpable conduct of the drill instructor, Staff Sergeant McKeon?

The seven officers heard from forty-four witnesses, including experts. Most of the witnesses were Marines ranging in rank from the privates involved in the exercise to experienced Marines testifying for the defense. The seven witnesses called by the defense included Marine Corps Commandant General Pate, who had convened the inquiry and resulting court-martial. General Pate was joined on the defense roster of witnesses by the most highly decorated member of the United States Marine Corps, Lt. Gen. Lewis B. Puller, Retired. Lt. Gen. Lewis B. Puller is one of only two men to have been awarded five Navy Crosses for valor in battle, and he is the only US Marine to have been so awarded, making him the most highly decorated officer in the Corps.

The trial began on July 16, 1956, and lasted just under four weeks, with the closing arguments on August 3, 1956. When Berman stood to begin his closing arguments, he was hopeful that all the hard work was behind him. His trial record was complete, brilliantly executed, and appeal ready, if necessary. He had masterfully cross-examined nineteen surviving privates with a gentle firmness that neither hurt nor exhibited any hardness toward them. He had presented expert testimony that showed the actual grade of the creek bed and thereby undermined anecdotal evidence of vastly varying depths within the creek and hearsay references to trout holes. He had submitted motion after motion in support of objections too numerous to outline. He had fought a good and honorable fight with a dignity and polite firmness now almost lost and foreign to modern judges and practitioners of the law.

Berman's tone was conversational, as it always was with juries. His voice was measured and tempered, except for in certain instances wherein he expressed a particular objection with a passion that skilled trial attorneys know as *budgeted emotion*. His approach was gentle and always gentlemanly. He wore a dark suit, perfectly pressed as they all had been throughout the trial, despite the near-hundred-degree heat in a room cooled only by an occasional fan and the faint breezes of humid swamps. His pants were creased and cuffed and fell precisely to the heel. His jacket sleeves fell right below the wrist. His suit had been hand-tailored to his small framed body that stood short of six feet. His eyes had a piercing, focused look through his wire-rim glasses. His initial introductory remarks began with an image of a living room, thereby invoking the many living rooms of citizens watching the trial:

> If I were to discuss this case with you, I would prefer to discuss it in an atmosphere of the living room of your home or mine, where I might sit down with you, both of us comfortable and neither of us formal, to tell, if I were there, what is the evidence in this case: that a fellow by the name of McKeon from very ordinary circumstances, who left high school after his second year at the tender age of seventeen to enlist in the navy in the defense of his country, and that through a period that he served of some forty months, speaking of kids—and kids have been referred to with great amplitude by trial counsel—that he served in combat, he performed his duties, he received an honorable discharge. In such circumstance, if we were talking in your living room or mine, wouldn't you have said, this is a good kid and he must have learned a lot from his experience? And if I went on in your living room in your home, to tell you there in that much more pleasant atmosphere what is evidence in this case, that this boy had a desire—maybe because his brothers had been Marines, maybe because he had been exposed to Marines in the Navy—a desire to become a Marine and to devote his career to it, so that he enlisted and reenlisted and presently is on his third enlistment, and that those various periods of practically his whole

adult life, his entire grown-up estate, had him performing duties both in combat, in training, and in teaching, and wherever he went, at whatever station or whatever theater anywhere, this man was well regarded, highly looked upon and, on each occasion of the expiration of his enlistment, honorably discharged. Is there one of you, in such an atmosphere, who would not have said: a good boy, a good dedicated Marine, and that your service needs men of that type, dedication, and devotion?

Now then, if I could continue on in your living room again without this formality of a courtroom and our legal rules, to say to you that this man, to enhance his career in the Marines, volunteered for a duty, which I believe somewhere along the line the evidence indicates not many volunteer for, the drill instructor school, and that ninety men in his class, who formed that class, but fifty-five graduated and that he stood fourteenth, and that moreover, if you took all of the men who ever have gone through drill instructor school for as far back as apparently records are available, his average of 84.9 was higher than the combined average of all the men who have gone through drill instructor school and that, when examined by these gentlemen who are qualified to make such examinations, under the modern methods of psychiatric observation, he was found to be highly motivated, stable, mature, and proficient... this isn't Berman talking; this is what I would say to you in your living room, which qualified men have said.

And then if I were to go on and say to you what is the evidence in this case that such a man, with such a reputation and with such grades and observations, is assigned to a platoon first, that he may not be the most articulate fellow in the world or even by any manner of means its greatest genius, but that he had a devotion to produce Marines, basic Marines. In fact, he even had a desire if it could have been accomplished to produce an honor platoon with men who were smart...well-disciplined, well-trained, independent Marines with that esprit de corps that makes this service different from any other service in our country. What would you then have said, all of you, as you sat here listening to what is the undisputed evidence in this case? That this is the true spirit of a good Marine and that he's been acting in the highest traditions of a devoted drill instructor? Now then, with this in mind, if I went on to tell you again in your living room that Sergeant McKeon—incidentally, a man of family, a man of decency, a man of devout religion, yes, even of warm humanity—found that this platoon of his, more than halfway through their training, not bad kids, no, but was lacking in discipline, that is to say actually not in discipline but lacking in that sharp discipline which is so necessary for the equipment of the men who are being prepared for war, and lacking in that spirit which is the heart of the esprit de corps so basic in every good Marine. And if I told you, confronted with that, despite his own affliction, that this man did not give up, he didn't become lackadaisical, he didn't adopt an indifferent attitude "Oh, what the hell do I care" attitude. Bound by his devotion to the Corps and by a New England conscience, he continued to attempt to perform his task. He kept trying using his own methods of trying to make basic Marines I say it is a fair intendment from the evidence that is before you, and I would say it to you in your own homes that if McKeon had turned this platoon out in their present state as described here, to take their places on ships and in stations in this Corps throughout the world and go into combat, his conscience would have hurt him to his dying day.

What would you have said in your homes, without getting into any emotionalism? Surely it would have been said that this is a good guy, this is good Marine. So if I went on to tell you, then, that in various ways and in various occasions and in various opportunities this man tried to teach discipline—this is a very broad field—he was going to undertake to do it, having not succeeded by other methods, by adopting a somewhat different and more rigorous exercise to teach more emphatically that so essential discipline and to instill in them that so lacking spirit. It seems to me that— well, it seems to me, I hope to you—that we would be called upon to forget everything that life has taught us…in fact, put aside our common sense completely.

If we didn't know that in dealing with this kind of a broad subject that the teaching of discipline and the instilling of spirit different men—not only in military establishment but all over, in every circumstance in life—respond differently and different organizations respond differently, and some method that might prove appropriate for one finds itself a singular failure for another. Then to hold, as apparently the trial counsel holds onto avidity, that in teaching discipline those who were charged with the performance of that task are exclusively confined to a lesson, a syllabus, a regulation or all of them, bespeaks a total lack of how men are taught and what is effective in teaching.

You do not have to take this alone from your own experience and your own common sense. You are not required to accept it because I say so. But surely two of the greatest experts in this Corps have offered that as their opinion.

Here, Berman referred to the judge's own commandant, General Pate, and Lt. Gen. Lewis B. Puller, Retired.

Well, now then, what was this rigorous exercise that this man was going to undertake with those tools for such a purpose? Trial counsel still talks in terms of punishment, punishment. He wanted them to get cold and wet. What about himself? What about himself? Isn't that the key to his entire motivation? Do you punish someone by subjecting yourself to whatever rigors are to be accomplished even when you are less physically fit than these who are supposed to be punished and oppressed? This is lawyer talk; this isn't talk that's handled in life where people meet to make decisions. What about this practice that obviously other drill instructors, probably from the time that this base was established, were confronted with the necessity of doing other things not contained in the syllabi or the lesson plans, that almost every drill instructor on this base knew that there was a practice for certain kinds of circumstances in teaching men discipline to take them into the boondocks or marshes or these creek waters. What for? For swimming lessons? For relaxation in an effort or an attempt to ford a creek? No, but to get through into different circumstances the hard "slodging," marching, to bring out order, discipline, and necessity on the part of the boys and make them men.

Berman reviewed the evidence in closing and then asked:

Does it require of Berman—I've never been a Marine, gentlemen, never—does it require me to tell you that it is good practice in the highest military tradition? You have your own experiences, and you have the opinion of the two great experts that I made mention of. Now, everybody now since this tragic event of April 8th, everyone now talks about these dangerous waters, about what lurking pitfalls there were, but what did people think about this before April 8th? Has there been one called to this stand, has there been a single regulation put in evidence, has there been a single statement made by anyone that up to April 8th, on Parris Island, Ribbon Creek was called a meandering little creek from which people fished? And that it was indeed. That there had never been a known drowning in any of the creeks around here? Now we suddenly find out these are tidal waters. Do you think that was known to the drill sergeants here, that these are tidal waters, not fresh water streams, that they have no openings? Now everyone suggests they have a current. Sure they have a current. Any time you have a tide you are bound to have some current, but the current that was measured here is a lesser current than you find in an ordinary stream, but it's a current, nevertheless. So now everyone speaks of these lurking dangers and pitfalls, and what Sergeant McKeon must have knowledge of. Why? Why? Where everybody on this base never recognized that there was any danger in those waters, where this place had never been put out of bounds, where no officer, no command ever told a single drill instructor: "Keep your people out of the marshes and creeks around this area, main side, battalion area, weapons area, except on this three-day hike and bivouac." Why not? Because no one here expected that there was any reasonable prospect of any dangers in the waters and marshes, including Ribbon Creek. But, nevertheless, both to show his leadership of his men and that he asked them to do nothing that he himself was not prepared to do, and also indeed to be the first to take that march in that mud and in those waters, so that as he put his feet down he would know whether there was any likelihood of danger to these troops that were following him. If you don't look upon things in the light of the after events, you'll find that his is a standard of care not only in the highest tradition of your Service but in the exercise of judgment.

What happened? It's an unhappy thing that's really a melancholy fact, gentlemen, that even with this trial no one, no one will ever know precisely what happened. We do know that there was an accident and that there was a panic, but I tell that this tragedy was not caused as a result of danger. It was not caused by any carelessness. It was not because of any wrongdoing, and it was not because of any heedlessness. The loss of these lives was due to panic.

Berman proceeded in his closing to review each element of the charges against Sergeant McKeon and ended by saying:

> I am almost through. I just ask for your tolerance and patience a brief few minutes more. The whole concept of justice, Officers of this court, demands that each man, each man receive his just due. We have a right. I say we have a right to expect a verdict of acquittal on Charges 2, 3, and 4 and along the specifications thereunder contained. Not because I stand here before you and ask for it, but because the evidence, the opinion of the outstanding experts, the facts, and the cause itself requires it. Indeed, because justice cried out for it.
>
> I have spent many, many weeks with my obligation and responsibility to Sgt. McKeon and to the United States Marine Corps. I have tried to serve them both well. At least to the best of my ability. At long last it comes to me to take this mantle of responsibility that I have carried heavily now for a long time and turn it over to you. You must assume that burden both for McKeon and the court. I am confident that you will deal well with each. You have my thanks for your patience in listening to me.[1]

The defense counsel returned to his seat next to the accused. His artful reference in the closing argument to a living room was a reminder to the presiding panel that a considerable amount of public opinion favorable to the defense had been spoken about and shaped in living rooms across the country by civilian and military Americans alike, many of whom were veterans of World War II, all of whom were following the trial. It was a case that was spoken of by almost every American because it was carried

---

1 Verbatim Record of Trial of Matthew C. McKeon by General Court Martial, Appointed by the Secretary of the Navy, July 16–August 4, 1956 (Department of the Navy, Office of the Judge Advocate General, Washington Navy Yard, Washington, DC), 862-869. Hereafter in the notes, this is referred to as "Trial Transcript."

by every newspaper in the country. To this day, it is a case that is still discussed, now mostly by Marines but occasionally still by family and friends associated with the events of April 8, 1956.

I heard about this case in one such living room of my parents' bayfront house on City Island, the home I grew up in and the home my father lived in for fifty-four years until he died in March of 2013. From his house on Tier Street, my father could see the Manhattan skyline to the south of Eastchester Bay and the Bronx. The city was out of his reach but not out of his sight, much like the years of his life working in New York City that were behind him but which remained in his mind's eye more vividly than the present. It was in my father's living room that he gave me his diary for 1956, photographs and the transcript of the court-of-inquiry proceedings that looked exactly as it did when he received it more than fifty years earlier, except the onion-skin paper was yellowed and the photos of the bodies that were once part of the record were removed by my mother many years ago.

By the time my father had given me his 1956 diary and the court-of-inquiry record, I had received from the United States Marine Corps both the court-of-inquiry and court-martial record on an electronic disk through my Freedom of Information Act (FOIA) request. The photos of the deceased were also not included in the FOIA record, most likely redacted from the record. The very photos of the deceased that the defense lawyers fifty years ago argued unsuccessfully to remove from the record as unnecessary and prejudicial were now removed from the record by the government. The government took too long, but in finally redacting the photos of the deceased from the trial record, it had nodded in late acquiescence to the defense argument that the photos added nothing to the proof and added too much to passions that do not serve justice well.

As a child, I found those photographs in a box attached to the onion-skin paper record of the court-of-inquiry proceedings that in 2012 my father gave me. They are gone now. My mother had hidden or threw them away since the time I accidently came across them so many years ago.

Those photos are not now part of any record of the proceedings. Posterity agreed with the defense counsel and removed them from every record.

My father's documents of the Ribbon Creek trial were pocketed in hiding places throughout the house I grew up in. An August 1956 *Life* magazine containing an article about my uncle was buried beneath meticulously pressed linen tablecloths in the dining-room hutch. Brig. Gen. William Baggarley McKean's 1958 memoir of the trial entitled *Ribbon Creek*, with its red binding and yellow cover, was in the far-back corner of the same hutch. My father's papers were in a box in a closet in the enclosed porch that surrounded his stucco-covered City Island house. My mother did her best to hide all references to Ribbon Creek, but it was among the very few tasks undertaken in her life that she failed at.

My discussion with my father of Ribbon Creek came late in his life, largely because my mother during her life would rarely speak of it or have it spoken of in her house. But on the few occasions she did speak of Ribbon Creek, she said that some recruits had been "horsing around," that some recruits had taunted others during the night exercise by crying "snakes" in a game-like tease to scare members of the platoon. Her tone was sad when she said it; her head hung low with her eyes to the ground as though trying to avoid the hopelessly impervious boundaries of history that touched past and future with a reach that would not be stayed.

My father's tone in speaking of the Ribbon Creek trial was similarly sad, but it was tempered by the assured satisfaction of work well done. He spoke to me about the Ribbon Creek trial as he sat in his living room on City Island in what became the last year of his life. The living room had a marble fireplace mantel to the right of double-glass doors that led from the dining room. In the center of the mantel was the US flag that had covered my mother's coffin in November 2004 and had been folded by the army in the triangular remembrance of her service in World War II. The army gave the flag to my father in a ceremony all armed forces repeat for all who have served a country made and sustained from the lives and deaths of the defenders of its constitution.

On either side of the flag on the mantel were pictures of my mother, my grandmother, and the Blessed Mother, Blessed Virgin Mary. The room was furnished with two Victorian chairs, each styled respectively in the decoration of royalty. One chair had lioness heads carved from wood lunging out from its arms, and its legs were carved as the feet of the lioness. The second chair had carved within its base the heads of a ram, and the legs were likewise that of a ram. A similarly ornately carved couch was pushed against a wall. His bed eventually replaced the lioness chair in the corner near the mantel, which gave the photographs of the mothers on the mantel an unobstructed view of my father as he slept.

New York newspapers littered the floor around a sturdy antique rocking chair that did not yield to his six-foot-two frame as he used his arms rather than weakening legs to get up. Thick reading glasses were frequently perched low on his nose so that he could look up to see the distance as he placed his paper on his lap or on the floor. The newspaper pile grew after my mother's death, pipe smoke permeated the rooms that had been previously forbidden to smoking, and he and I spoke of the Ribbon Creek trial.

The discussion was prompted by the gift of a book about Ribbon Creek that was given to me by my husband's colleague, Jodi. My husband and Jodi were both working with Marines in Parris Island in civilian-advisory capacities. My interest in the trial stemmed as much from the law of the case as from its history. My father was and I am a member in good standing of the Bar of the State of New York: he for fifty years, I for twenty-seven years. I am also a member in good standing of the Bar of North Carolina. The law became a bond with my father that I found later in life. The law gave me a prism through which I could see a life I had previously misunderstood and underestimated as many children do until age enlarges their perspective. This story is my bond to how my father and the lawyers in his day were able to practice law in a manner now diminished from the law, and it is my connection to lives now lost to me.

It is also a record of a significant part my parents' lives and their role in the criminal defense of my uncle, Sgt. Matthew McKeon. It is the record of a defense that started with my parents and then found unexpected help from members of the New York State Bar and the New York State Bench. New York lawyers and judges volunteered without compensation to assist in the defense of Sergeant McKeon in a way worth remembering now, in a way my father said he had not seen before or after in all his fifty-six years in the practice of law.

The defense included a New York State Supreme Court judge, who after reading about the court-of-inquiry proceedings formed a committee to aid in the defense of Sergeant McKeon. Judge James B. McNally was the honorary chairman of this committee, and he asked Berman to be a member. Berman was a leading trial attorney in the City of New York in 1956 and had recently prevailed in a personal-injury case awarding a then record jury verdict of three hundred thousand dollars. When Judge McNally asked Berman to be a member of that committee, Berman said, "I will not only be a member; I'll try the case." Berman volunteered and became the lead counsel on the court-martial. Judge Walter Lynch served as co-chairman on the committee. Supreme Court Referees Cohalon McGuhan; Wyatt of Sullivan and Cromwell, Downey, Whelan; and Mannix of White and Case served as members on the committee, as well as my father.

A defense team of additional civilian and military lawyers reviewed transcripts, law, and rules of procedure for court-martials. They conducted interviews, and they wrote letters to former Marines and traveled to different cities in an effort to identify potential witnesses who had come through Parris Island and had underwent similar training exercises as the one Sergeant McKeon conducted. They searched tirelessly for witnesses, and their efforts were rewarded by the cooperation and testimony of retired Lt. Gen. Lewis B. Puller, who is known as "Chesty" to the Marines and to his family.

This is a story about the law and lawyers as told to me by my father in his City Island house. His dark brown eyes were set deeply in his face, and his right brow would arch as though to confirm his certitude as he remembered a case where his education, his law license, his community, his city, and his colleagues came together to work for his family. It is a case he remembered well and a case that Marine history will not forget.

The telling of it in my father's voice will begin in Calvary Hospice in the Bronx on November 11, 2004, the day my mother died.

CHAPTER ONE

––––

A TRIPLE WINDOW OF THE Calvary Hospice room of my wife, Anne Margaret McKeon Costello, frames what was once our lives here in the Bronx where Anne and I lived. We lived almost forgotten lives until today, when death remembered us with a whisper that called for Anne and left behind sixty-five years of our lives together. We are not unwitnessed and alone in our life or in our death, or so it seems this morning on November 11, 2004, Veterans Day. Today, Anne's life ended on the very same date and almost to the minute of the death last year of her brother Matthew McKeon, on November 11, 2003.

As I look out the window onto unstoried Bronx buildings, I see that a few miles north is our home on City Island. To my southeast is the cemetery off Tremont Avenue where my parents and sister are buried. They were all laid out for visitation at McNulty's Funeral Home in Pelham Bay, Bronx, slightly northeast of Calvary. Anne's wake will likewise be at McNulty's before her final trip to Cherry Valley, Massachusetts, where she will be buried at St. Joseph's with her brothers, including Matthew McKeon, and with her sisters, parents, and grandparents. McNulty's Funeral Home sits on the very spot where my father's tavern once stood on Middletown Road in the Bronx. It was called the Emerald Isle Tavern. As I look out this window at the places we have lived and died, I wonder what part of what I see—what streetlamp, building, street, or sidewalks—will remember the sound of our

1

voices or sight of our footprints that tell our story, along with the ebb and flow of those who will come and live here after us.

There is nothing ahead to answer me but the elevated train moving southeast toward Manhattan, branding an invisible track of the path our lives have taken into a silent memory. Silence answers me and records why it was Matthew McKeon who came for Anne today. It was his last call to duty to come back here to Calvary and walk Anne to the place where there is finally forgiveness for all and for the events that took place on April 8, 1956, that led to Matt's court-martial that summer—events for which in 1956, Emile Zola Berman, lead counsel for the defense of Sergeant McKeon at the court-martial, asked in his closing remarks: "What happened? It's an unhappy thing that's really a melancholy fact, gentlemen, that even with this trial no one, no one will ever know precisely what happened. We do know that there was an accident and that there was a panic." Panic.

These are the facts as best I can tell them, both melancholy and unknowable, that bring the coincidence of the death on a Veterans Day to both sister and brother who were veterans of World War II. Many may not agree on every detail, but I, Brig. Gen. William Baggarley McKean, the United States Marine Corps commanding officer of weapons battalion in 1956, and Emile Zola Berman, defense counsel for Matthew McKeon, squarely agree on this: no one would ever know precisely what happened on the night of April 8, 1956, in Ribbon Creek. Brigadier General McKean put it a little differently than Counselor Berman. McKean's assessment as recorded in his 1958 book, *Ribbon Creek,* was that there was in Ribbon Creek "a different sort of panic and these survivors perceived themselves in spectators' roles because they didn't get mixed up in the melee…trying to dovetail observations of the Ribbon Creek panic is a different matter: Ultimate truth washed out on the ebbing tide that very night."[2]

The night of April 8, 1956, in Ribbon Creek, Parris Island, can be pieced together from the trial and inquiry transcripts, but not completely.

---

2 Brigadier General William B. McKean, *Ribbon Creek* (New York: The Dial Press, 1958), 209-210.

What can be said for sure is that a panic broke out in the platoon that resulted in the death of six young Marine Corps recruits: Thomas Curtis Hardeman, Donald Francis O'Shea, Charles Francis Reilly, Jerry Lamonte Thomas, Leroy Thompson, and Norman Alfred Wood. Panic is the second point that Counselor Berman and Brig. Gen. McKean agreed on in their statements about that night.

Over fifty years ago, we all tried to fully understand the events of that night. I am going to try again. As I write what happened, forgive my footnotes, but the record itself is what I can know for sure and how I can know it.

———

On Sunday morning, April 8, 1956, my wife's younger brother, S. Sgt. Matthew McKeon, was a Marine Corps drill instructor on Parris Island, South Carolina. He was assigned to his first platoon and had weekend duty on that date. He was thirty-one years old and had spent almost half his life in the United States Navy and then the US Marines. He was tall and thin, his fair hair cut in the short fashion of his service. He had the same bright blue in his eyes as Anne and as that of a clear sky. They both had the same wide smile and looked more alike than their other siblings. He was married with two young children and a third on the way. His wife, Betty McKeon, was beautiful with jet-black, short hair, high cheekbones, and an olive complexion.

Sergeant McKeon was an experienced combat veteran and teacher, training Marines in the use of weapons in combat, but that weekend he was the junior drill sergeant on duty. Platoon Seventy-One was served by Senior Drill Instructor Sergeant Huff, Junior Drill Instructor Sergeant King, and Sergeant McKeon. King and McKeon were recent graduates from drill-instructor school.

Staff Sergeant McKeon's training as a drill instructor had begun three months earlier in January 1956 at drill-instructor school. He and all the other drill instructors attending learned that a Marine recruit goes through four mental stages. These four mental stages were described in exhibit twenty of the court-of-inquiry record and were relied upon by the attorneys trying to understand what happened and how it happened. It started in training.

Court of Inquiry, Exhibit Twenty, was entitled: "Lesson Number One, the Psychology of the Recruits, Drill Instructor School, dated January 1955." The four mental stages a recruit experiences are shock and fear, awakening, reasoning, and group association.[3] In the early stages of training, recruits go through a stage taught at drill-instructor school in 1956 known as the *shock-and-fear* stage. After signing a contract, a recruit will find himself on a bus or train headed to Yemassee, South Carolina, where he will be met by "salty" yelling orders to someone called "you." "You" cannot smoke unless a smoking lamp is lit. "You" get on a bus to a receiving station and are referred to by last name only. "You" do not understand the military terms and are confused and disoriented. The recruit meets his drill sergeant, who introduces himself and states firmly: "*I* am in charge."

The platoon has a number. Every "you" is told to get behind one another, but the new platoon members are all standing too close together. They are warned to stay in that position and begin marching, which causes them to step on one another's feet. They are marched out onto parade grounds so they can observe better-trained platoons marching closely and in step. They begin to doubt if they can ever do that, and then they are taken to "hygienic," where they are stripped and checked for body lice, and begin to feel slightly disrespected. Then the "final blow" comes: all their hair is cut off, and they all look alike and they are in shock, "really in shock." They

---

3 Record of Proceedings of a Court of Inquiry, "into the circumstances surrounding the marching of Platoon 71, third Recruit Training Battalion, into the swamps adjacent to the Weapons Training Battalion on April 8, 1956, and the disappearance of Private Thomas Curtis Hardeman, 1587021, USMC; Private First Class Donald Francis O'Shea, 1550900, USMC; Private Charles Francis Reilly, 1566628, USMC; Private Jerry Lamonte Thomas, 1585496, USMC; Private Leroy Thompson, 1590031, USMC; and Private Norman Alfred Wood, 1590034, USMC" (Department of the Navy, Office of the Judge Advocate General, Alexandria, Virginia, April 1956), Exhibit Twenty. Hereafter in the notes, this is referred to as "Court of Inquiry Transcript."

are subdivided into squads. There is no social standing; all of them, regardless of background, look alike. At this point, that recruit called "you" is "a very confused lad."[4]

The period of *awakening* comes in the second or third week when the recruit pays closer attention to the drill instructor. Next comes the period of *reasoning* in the third or fourth week when the recruits ask questions to better understand and absorb their training. They no longer do things out of fear, but they follow orders out of understanding. Their pride in appearance improves. Their pride as a Marine increases as their understanding increases. Finally, in the final weeks of training comes the *group association* wherein the recruit wants to do well for the good of the platoon and wants to be the best in competition.[5] It was this last phase of coming together as a group that Platoon Seventy-One had not reached, in spite of the best efforts of their trainers. In April 1956, their trainers only had a few more weeks to bring this platoon together.

Platoons were numbered sequentially as they formed in a calendar year.[6] Platoon Seventy-One began on February 23, 1956. Platoon Seventy-One's roster took up three sheets of paper, upon which was noted the names of eighty-five recruits.[7] There had been seventy platoons preceding them. Their roster included the names of six men who were transferred in from Platoon Fifty-Nine because "they had been slow learners."[8] Those six were Thomas Hardeman, Lester Hendrix, Richard Acker, Marvin Blair, Mims Brower, and Charles Reilly.[9] Jerry Lamonte Thomas had been in Platoon Sixty-Seven but lost time in sick bay, joining Platoon Seventy-One on February 29, 1956, the same date as the six "slow learners."[10] Shortly thereafter, two were transferred out due to illiteracy, three were transferred

---

4 Court of Inquiry Transcript, Exhibit Twenty.

5 Ibid.

6 McKean, *Ribbon Creek*, 50.

7 Trial Transcript, Prosecution Exhibit Fourteen.

8 McKean, *Ribbon Creek*, 51.

9 Trial Transcript, 679, Prosecution Exhibit Fourteen.

10 Ibid.; McKean *Ribbon Creek*, 51.

due to lost time in sick bay, and a fourth joined the platoon. By April 8, 1956, the platoon numbered seventy-nine.[11]

The roster of Platoon Seventy-One began with Acker and continued with names such as Grabowski, Geckle, Golden, Delgado, Martinez, Johnson, Keaton, Langone, McGuire, Moran, Mulligan, O'Rourke, O'Shea, Serantes, Sygman, Rogers, Vaughn, Veney, and Whitmore. They came from cities, both north and south, and from the mountains and coasts of the eastern part of the United States. They were white of European origin, black of African American origin, and Hispanic. They were Catholic, Jewish, and Protestant. They were diverse and had not yet formed a cohesive unit in their training.

The young men from the cities were at the greatest disadvantage in their ability to navigate the low country of South Carolina. A city is always lit, even if dimly, from its collective night lights, in a way that a country night cannot rival with its fullest moon. Country nights are blindingly dark compared with a city night. The ground is also unfamiliar. The yielding soft soils of the country are unpredictably opposite to the firm concrete sidewalks and streets of a city. These differences underscored the almost impossible chore of unifying northerners and southerners, as well as blacks, whites, and Hispanics, and this collectively worked against the men of Platoon Seventy-One in April of 1956.

Platoon Seventy-One met the early challenges of its training. From March 1 to March 24, they endured long hours of drill, equipment training, and lectures. They slept together, ate together, and did everything together. On March 24, the platoon was moved from Nissen Huts in the third battalion area to rifle range. They were housed in the northeast corner of the lower-deck squad bay in Building 761. The first two weeks of rifle range were grueling. Reveille would sound at 4:30 a.m. They would police up, get breakfast, and be on the school range by 6:45 a.m. On the range they were required to get into difficult positions to shoot, straining their

---

11 Ibid.

muscles from their shoulders to their fingers.[12] Their bodies and strained muscles would have been exhausted.

Platoon Seventy-One's nights on rifle range were spent in swimming instruction wherein qualification was determined by navigating a mere two laps in the pool, some by dog paddle. Several young men found the dog paddle difficult, not because it required much more than simple management of water, but because it required any management of water. Any swimming stroke, even a childlike dog paddle, requires eradication of fear of the water. Fear became their worst enemy on the night of April 8, 1956.

Sunday, April 8, 1956, began between 5:00 a.m. and 5:30 a.m.[13] Pain in Sergeant McKeon's back ran down his left leg and into his toe. He could not bend his toe without feeling the pain run down his hip all the way down his leg, stiffening his leg muscle. It was a severe pain that had been bothering him for three weeks and left him visibly limping through his duties. Three weeks earlier he had been diagnosed with a herniated lumbar disc with nerve impingement. In an attempt to relieve the pressure on the nerves in his back, he walked with a makeshift cane fashioned from a squeegee mop handle.[14] He did anything he could but quit. Marines don't quit.

Sergeant McKeon attended Catholic mass after working approximately 132 hours in the week that had past.[15] Father Bieliski presided over the mass and would later that night find himself praying again for this very group in front of him. Sergeant McKeon left mass early to get the Protestant members of his platoon to breakfast or "chow" by 7:15 a.m. Before leaving mass, he assigned a section leader for the platoon, Langone, to see that the Catholics went back to mess hall after mass. He checked into mess hall by signing in the number of his platoon (Seventy-One), his initial, and the number of Catholics who would be eating after services. He ate breakfast and sat and talked with his fellow drill instructors until heading back to

---

12 McKean, *Ribbon Creek,* 61.

13 Trial Transcript, 697.

14 Ibid., 700–1.

15 Ibid., 182–83.

Building 761 where his platoon was assigned.[16] After breakfast approximately fifty-five Protestants in the platoon shoved off with another recruit in charge of their church detail.[17] Sergeant McKeon went upstairs to where a fellow drill instructor, Sergeant Muckler, was "billeted" with his platoon. They continued the conversation they had started at breakfast and then returned to his barracks to check in with Recruit Langone and tell Langone to make sure that all laundry was done and gear was clean.[18]

Sergeant McKeon's morning conversation with his fellow drill instructors was filled with talk of Platoon Seventy-One's weak performance in marksmanship. Sergeant Scarborough, who was the instructor for Rifle Range at Parris Island, said he had taken a platoon through Rifle Range every three weeks since last fall and seen every platoon since then, and Platoon Seventy-One was the worst platoon he had seen. In fact, he said it was "piss poor."[19] It appeared to Sergeant McKeon that Sergeant Scarborough was "pee'd off at them."[20] Worse, it seemed he was failing, and Marines do not fail.

Sergeant Scarborough asked McKeon if he had any liquor around. Sergeant Scarborough was feeling pretty rough from the previous Saturday night and thought it was just the sort of pained morning to make a man angry over a poor platoon and thirsty for the relief only another drink can bring. Sergeant McKeon did not have any booze. It was not his habit to keep booze around barracks. But Sergeant Scarborough remembered he had a bottle of vodka in his car with a little leftover from the previous night. He asked Sergeant McKeon to drive him to get it, which Sergeant McKeon did. They returned to the barracks with a bottle of vodka that had a little more than a fifth left in it. There was not that much left after a Saturday night that finished with a need for more.

---

16   Ibid.
17   Ibid., 698.
18   Ibid., 699.
19   McKean, *Ribbon Creek*, 92.
20   Trial Transcript, 702.

Before either Sergeants McKeon or Scarborough had had a shot of the vodka, Sergeant Muckler came in and asked, "Whose platoon is out there crapped out on the lawn out in the back of the barracks?"[21]

Sergeant McKeon said it could not be his because he had personally seen them earlier following his orders cleaning and doing laundry.

But Sergeant Muckler smiled, amused at the overconfidence and misplaced faith in the platoon, and said, "I think it is yours."

First Sergeant Scarborough had complained about the platoon in rifle range, and now Sergeant Muckler had come in echoing the lack of discipline in his platoon. Sergeant McKeon was incredulous—it had to be a mistake. He rushed to the back door to see for himself. Sergeant Scarborough followed behind him. Approximately fifteen to twenty members of Platoon Seventy-One were lying on the grass.[22] They were lying on their backs, some with their heads resting in their hands with elbows bent, others with their arms crossed across the ground. A section leader of Platoon Seventy-One, Recruit Butler, was sitting on the steps with some others writing letters. Letter writing was a permitted Sunday activity, but the failure to admonish the others on the lawn exhibited a lack of leadership. Sergeant McKeon ordered the recruits to get inside barracks.

Private Butler asked Sergeant McKeon if he and the few sitting with him could finish writing their letters. This small group of African American recruits had obeyed orders and just wanted to finish their letters. Among them, a private wrote to his mother that day that he could not describe how bad it was in Parris Island. The next morning, the private was dead. His letter went out in the mail and reached his mother midweek.

Sergeant McKeon saw failure and a pervasive lack of unity in his first platoon. His answer of no came quickly, and he reprimanded Private Butler: "What kind of nonsense is this, you being a section leader and

---

21 Ibid., 705.
22 Ibid., 702, 751.

letting this go on? Don't you see those people out there lying around?" Sergeant McKeon again ordered everyone inside.[23]

Platoon Seventy-One entered their barracks and stood by their beds as Sergeant McKeon wondered how to fix this problem of a lack of discipline and unity among them. He considered a rifle exercise—up and on shoulders, right arm first, right hand first—but if they got tired and one of the rifles hit the racks, then it would knock the data off the rifle.[24] He ordered a field day instead, a day of cleaning and chores.

When Sergeant McKeon returned to the drill instructors' room, Sergeant Scarborough was having a drink from that bottle they retrieved earlier. He offered a drink to Sergeant McKeon, who said he could not drink it straight. Sergeant McKeon went up to Sergeant Muckler's room and got a Coke. When he returned, Sergeant McKeon took a swig from the vodka bottle and chased it with Coke.[25] They remained there approximately one hour talking, which included some talk about how to improve Platoon Seventy-One. As they sat, Sergeant King came into the room. Sergeant McKeon and Sergeant King had a drink. That was Sergeant McKeon's second drink.[26]

Sergeant Scarborough wanted to head down to the noncommissioned officers (NCO) club, and he asked Sergeant McKeon for a ride. Sergeant King agreed to take Platoon Seventy-One to lunch if Sergeant McKeon was back by 2:00 p.m. Sergeant McKeon figured he could take Scarborough to the NCO club and pick up the mail. Before they left the drill instructors' room, Sergeant McKeon said to Sergeant Scarborough: "Here, Gunny, here is your bottle. Take it with you."

Sergeant Scarborough responded, "Leave it here. I'll pick it up later." It was ten minutes to one when they left.[27]

---

23 Ibid., 703.
24 Ibid.
25 Ibid., 706.
26 Ibid., 707.
27 Ibid., 350–4, 713.

The responsibility of the recruits weighed heavily on Sergeant McKeon as he drove to pick up the mail, and he thought of something his senior drill sergeant had said to Platoon Seventy-One. He recalled Sergeant Huff saying, "I chewed their tails one day and told them that if they don't snap out of their hockey, I would take them in the swamps."[28] He knew the only reason Sergeant Huff had not done that yet was that he had not found the time in the busy training schedule.[29] Sergeant McKeon thought a march in the marshes would instill discipline as it had done for Sergeant McKeon in his own Parris Island training so many years ago and as it had done for so many Marines so many times in the past.

Sergeants McKeon and Scarborough entered the NCO club together, but someone called Sergeant Scarborough to his table, so he separated from Sergeant McKeon, who went over to the bar and ordered a Schlitz beer. He poured the beer into a glass and took a few sips before he noticed a friend at the other end of the bar. He left the glass of beer and went over to his friend, Shoup. Sergeant McKeon said, "Congratulations, I heard you made master."

Shoup responded, "I did. Thank you. Tell you what, I'll buy a drink for every stripe I have made since I saw you last."

Shoup then turned to the bartender: "A triple shot of whiskey over here." Shoup had been a buck sergeant when Sergeant McKeon last saw him and had earned three stripes since then.

Shoup and Sergeant McKeon both stood among the crowd around the bar. Sergeant McKeon reached over and lifted the triple shot of whiskey. He took a sip out of gratitude: "Here is luck to you." (Sergeant McKeon preferred beer to liquor.)[30] He then put the unfinished shot down on the bar as Shoup talked about his new car. They left their drinks at the crowded bar and went out to the parking lot to see the car.[31] When Shoup and

---

28 Court of Inquiry Transcript, 129; Trial Transcript, 175-76.
29 Trial Transcript, 179.
30 Ibid., 710.
31 Ibid., 711.

Sergeant McKeon returned inside, it was twenty minutes to two. Sergeant McKeon retrieved the glass of Schlitz he had left at the bar intending to chase the whiskey down with it. He then walked over to where he had left the triple shot, but when he returned the whiskey was gone. There were several men standing where he had left the whiskey, and he figured they drank it, mixing theirs up with his. Sergeant McKeon took a few sips of the beer and realized the hour. He had to leave to get back to King, who was scheduled to go on liberty at 2:00 p.m.[32] That was the last drink of alcohol Sergeant Matthew McKeon ever drank in his life.

When Sergeant McKeon returned to Parris Island with the mail, he saw members of Platoon Seventy-One playing a game of chicken in the grass.[33] More nonsense, more bull hockey, and more reason for more training, he thought as he told a recruit to retrieve the mail from the trunk of his car. Sergeant McKeon lay down and dozed off thinking about what to do with his platoon. Recruit Langone woke him up at ten minutes to five for chow. He washed and put on a jacket. At approximately twenty after five, he told Langone that the troops should fall out in ten minutes. At five thirty, the troops marched to mess hall.[34]

Platoon Seventy-One was the last platoon on the mess-hall schedule that night out of the twenty-eight platoons on Parris Island in April of 1956. The call for seconds came unluckily to them, because Sergeant Huff had expressed that the platoon should not go in for seconds if they were firing. It was Huff's belief that if "men are fat and if they go back for seconds they cannot get in proper position to fire a rifle."[35] In spite of having been told by their senior drill sergeant not to indulge in seconds, Langone rose from the mess table and passed the drill sergeant's table on his way to get seconds.

Sergeant McKeon asked Langone: "Where are you going?"

---

32 Ibid.
33 Ibid., 702–13.
34 Ibid., 713.
35 Trial Transcript, 160.

Langone responded, "I am going for seconds."

"Why?"

"Because I am hungry."

"What did you do today to deserve seconds?"

Langone answered sarcastically, "What do I have to do to be hungry?"

As Langone continued past his drill sergeant for second helpings in defiance of earlier instructions not to do so when in shooting practice, Sergeant McKeon stood up and said, "I want to see you in my room when I get back to barracks."[36]

After dinner, the Catholics went to novena, and the Protestants went to hymn singing. Those men wishing to participate in evening services had just ten minutes to eat and get down to the liaison office to get transportation to the main side for church services.[37] When the remainder returned to barracks at Building 761, Sergeant McKeon ordered a second field day because the recruits knew that they were not supposed to have seconds while at the range, yet they went in for seconds anyway.[38] He also spoke with the section leaders separately.

Sergeant McKeon called Langone first and told him he better come in swinging. Langone declined the offer. McKeon asked, "Did you ever hit your mother or father?"

"No, sir, I never did."

"Why haven't you?"

"Because I respect them?"

"Don't you respect your superior officers as well?"

"Yes, sir."

"Well, was that any respect you showed me in the mess hall this evening?" As Sergeant McKeon said that, he slapped him lightly on the side of the head, not to hurt him but to illustrate that he had not acted respectfully.

Langone apologized. "I am sorry I sounded off in there."

---

36   Ibid., 315, 713.

37   Ibid., 714.

38   Ibid., 714–15.

Sergeant McKeon leaned against a table and told Langone to sit down. He offered him a cigarette. He asked Langone:

Do you realize the responsibility you have in that platoon? Do you realize the duties of a section leader? It is to act as a liaison between the platoon and drill instructor. It is to show an example of discipline. Here you are as a section leader and you are goofing off as much as those other kids. When those kids see you goofing naturally they are going to follow you.[39]

The main thing of the Marines is discipline. Without discipline you have nothing. The very purpose of recruit training here is discipline. The purpose of training here is not to go out of here being an honor student more or less, but to go out of here with good discipline. Some day you may be called up to defend this country of ours, to defend your home and without discipline you will have nothing. If you ever carry this discipline throughout the Marine Corps with you it will save your life if you do get into combat and if you don't have it you will be shipped home in a box.[40]

Langone seemed to understand and appeared genuinely sorry he had not worked harder, and he promised to do better and help everyone get "squared away." Sergeant McKeon asked him to send in Maloof and Private Wood. Maloof came in sloppily, and Sergeant McKeon slapped him lightly to show his disapproval. He asked, "Is that the position of attention?"

"No, sir." Maloof straightened himself out as he said it.

"Why don't you two big guys slam each other? Why don't you fight like that game of chicken you were playing? Go ahead."

"No, sir."

It was not such a good idea now. Sergeant McKeon turned to Wood and said, "Just because you are colored, Wood, there is no difference between

---

39 Ibid., 716.
40 Ibid.

you and the other people in the platoon. None whatsoever. Your actions distinguish you, nothing else."

He said to both Maloof and Wood who were tall men: "You people are goofing off as much as these little guys in there, and when you people goof off those little guys are going to goof off. What you get away with, they will get away with."

Both Recruits Maloof and Wood agreed that they had been slacking off since they were assigned to the range. Sergeant McKeon asked them to promise to instill some discipline. He said: "I want you both to stop your friends from goofing off. Go up and talk to them if you see them goofing off and ask, 'What are you doing that for?' I want you to go out there and stop them from fooling around. Beat them if you have to, but stop the goofing. What those little guys are doing...they are only following your example. Whatever they do, it not only throws reflection on themselves but on the whole platoon."[41]

Sergeant McKeon continued: "Being a Marine was not just wearing a uniform and getting their pay every two weeks and going on liberty and having a gay time. A Marine basically has one primary job, and that is regarding fighting and learning to fight and learning to put themselves in a position both physically and mentally and preparing themselves for someday, who knows when; preparing themselves for the day of combat, not just a day of putting on a uniform and getting paid every two weeks."[42]

Later Maloof recalled that Sergeant McKeon wanted to make an honor platoon out of them. He asked these men that night to sharpen their responsibilities to the platoon, to act like leaders.[43] The men were tall, and McKeon reasoned to them both that a smaller man would listen to a taller man.[44] He spoke about discipline. He told them that the purpose of the exercise was to instill discipline. He told Maloof:

---

41 Ibid., 718–19.
42 Ibid., 719.
43 Ibid., 264.
44 Ibid.

"I want this to be an honor platoon. I want to instill discipline. Discipline is the most important lesson you will take out of here." Maloof remembered Sgt. McKeon said that: "In combat an undisciplined platoon could mean death to the whole platoon, and not just one man. Whoever it was that was goofing off could cause the whole platoon to get knocked off."[45]

Sergeant McKeon then talked to them of what life in the Marines would be like after boot camp. He spoke to them of the West Coast Marines and about his life in the Marines. He was cordial in his natural and friendly manner. As they parted, he said to Maloof and Wood lightheartedly, "Now get out of here and send someone else in."[46]

Maloof believed Sergeant McKeon was attempting to instill the seriousness of training. He accepted the guidance and agreed to become more serious, to become a leader. He promised himself to become the Marine he signed up to become, an honor Marine, and he did.[47]

The next recruit was McPherson. McPherson was one of the tallest and biggest men in the platoon at six feet three inches tall and approximately 175 pounds. He was also one of the more popular men in the platoon, and many of the men looked up to him.[48] He appeared to his superior officers in every way to be a pretty good young man. He had common sense—so much so that Sergeants Huff, King, and McKeon had put him on the finances of the platoon. McPherson was in charge of the money the platoon got for laundry and the cobbler shop. Sergeant McKeon now had another task for McPherson: one of assuming a larger leadership role with the group.[49]

As McPherson walked toward Sergeant McKeon's room, he saw him waiting for him in the hallway. McPherson entered the room after being

---

45 Ibid.
46 Ibid., 253.
47 Ibid., 265.
48 Ibid., 353.
49 Ibid., 720.

called in by Sergeant McKeon and stood at attention. Sergeant McKeon asked him, "What is wrong with you? You are acting like an individual out there. Why aren't you doing something to help the platoon with better discipline?"

He answered, "I am just a recruit like the rest. All I can help is myself."

Sergeant McKeon slapped McPherson with the back of his hand and asked him, "Is that your attitude?" Sergeant McKeon had a look of disbelief on his face when he asked that, a look of frustration. He told McPherson to sit down.[50]

McPherson sat against a locker back next to the bunk, which was immediately to his right. Sergeant McKeon then said: "The Marines do not work as individuals; they work together as one unit. The platoon lacks discipline, and I don't know why. Do you know why? What can be done to change the discipline and team spirit of the platoon?"

McPherson responded, "The platoon has had it too easy right from the beginning." McPherson believed then and after that it was a poorly disciplined platoon that had no spirit at all. They worked individually and never worked together.

Sergeant McKeon said, "If they have it too easy, what if they didn't? What do you think if we march into the boondocks? Do you think that would be a good idea?"

McPherson replied, "Yes, sir, that is a good idea. It could change the discipline."

Sergeant McKeon then told McPherson:

I have seen a lot of platoons in my fifteen years of service, I have seen some with so much spirit that when the bullets and bombs are flying they have so much spirit they make it through, they survive, they live to tell about it. I have seen others with less discipline and no spirit and they don't make it. If this platoon were in combat now it would not make it. They would not come home.[51]

---

50 Ibid.
51 Trial Transcript, 350

As Sergeant McKeon said this, his mind seemed to wander to the troops who did not make it, to a home that might not have been there to return to but for the troops who fought: some who made it and others who did not. He thought of Korea and of the USS *Essex*. He thought a night march would help. He thought of men and boys becoming men, and boys who never got the chance to become men. He thought of the bottle Scarborough left. He thought it was at times like these that made a man thirsty. He walked over to the bottle and picked it up from the floor where it sat next to a desk. He lifted it, the cap still on. He asked, "Do you drink vodka, McPherson?"

"I have."

"Do you like vodka?"

"Yes."

"So you think it is good stuff?"

"I do."

"Do you want a drink?"

"It is up to you, sir."

Sergeant McKeon put the bottle to his lips, cap still on, as though to drink, but he did not. McPherson did not see the cap come off and saw no other evidence of a man drinking. He did not see a swallow. He did not hear a swish or sound of liquid. He did not see the liquid diminish in amount. He could not say that McKeon drank at all, only that he lifted the bottle and put it down. He observed nothing more, nothing less.[52]

The cap remained on as Sergeant McKeon said to McPherson, attempting to make a point he would later regret: "When you prove to me you are a man, then you can take a drink."[53]

Sergeant McKeon would recall this later as a poor gesture. It was indeed a poor gesture, but it came from a man whose only education was in the battlefield. His only desk was a hill with machine guns pointed at an enemy who wanted to take his country and his life. His only academy was

---

52   Ibid., 207, 354, 402, 419.
53   Ibid., 350, 351, 720.

the USS *Essex*, now acclaimed for its legendary service. It was all he had to offer Platoon Seventy-One, and it was all he knew to give them to forge discipline and unity in them.

At 8:00 p.m. and 8:30 p.m. that night, Sergeant McKeon entered the barracks of Building 761. They were in the middle of their field day, cleaning. Some had just recently returned from novena and hymn singing. They were wearing their boots, dungaree jackets, and utility jackets, and some had sweatshirts underneath.[54] Word had gotten out to the platoon that they were headed to the boondocks. Everybody was feeling pretty good about it. They were in high spirits. They thought it was a pretty good idea. There was a general feeling of joy when the call came from Sergeant McKeon.[55]

Fall out.

Platoon Seventy-One fell out in front of the barracks. Sergeant McKeon stood in front of the platoon, leaning on his makeshift cane for support. He said, "We are going into the swamps, we are going swimming, and those of you who cannot swim will drown and the rest will be eaten by sharks."[56] They thought that was funny. They laughed.[57] They took it as a joke.[58]

Sergeant McKeon marched with a noticeable limp, supporting each step with the wooden handle of the squeegee mop.[59] Right face. Forward march. They marched down the small road leading to the rifle range. Column half right. They crossed the street. Column right. They marched parallel to the Able and Baker Ranges.[60] A sprinkler was spraying water near a small building. Some walked around it. In an effort to cut out the laughing and joking, Sergeant McKeon said, "Go through it," and most of them did.[61]

---

54 Ibid., 199.
55 Ibid., 253; Court of Inquiry Transcript, 93.
56 Court of Inquiry Transcript, 40–41.
57 Trial Transcript, 196.
58 Ibid., 237.
59 Ibid., 209.
60 Court of Inquiry Transcript, 20.
61 Trial Transcript, 197.

Column right. They marched behind Charlie Butts. Column left. They marched toward the water of Ribbon Creek behind Charlie Butts. As they walked through the grass headed for the creek, Sergeant McKeon yelled, "Watch out for snakes," and he pushed the reeds in front of his step with his walking stick to keep his own eye out for snakes.[62]

Platoon Seventy-One started little by little to break ranks and fall into small groups with friends.[63] They were still joking as they neared the water and continued joking as they entered the water. By the time they reached the water's edge, they were in groups of four and five; they were not in formation.[64] Later, testifying under oath, Recruit Joseph Anthony Moran would recall: "If everybody had stayed in ranks and followed Sergeant McKeon, nothing would have happened, because the men that were near him were all right, sir."[65]

Platoon Seventy-One marched, and some joked and some sang as they trudged through the mud on the edge of Ribbon Creek. They all believed this exercise was a lark. They thought if they went in the water, it would be up to their waist. They thought the purpose was to show them the drill sergeant meant business and then they would have discipline.[66] They were fooling around the entire time.[67] There was nobody scared at first; they thought it was pretty funny.[68] Some were singing.[69] They exchanged wise-cracks and were having fun.[70] Sergeant McKeon told them more than once to knock off the joking.[71] They did not listen.

They entered the waters of Ribbon Creek. Column right. They walked along the mud directly parallel to the edge of the creek for approximately

---

62 Ibid., 197, 215.
63 Court of Inquiry Transcript, 16.
64 Trial Transcript, 387–89.
65 Court of Inquiry Transcript, 11.
66 Trial Transcript, 200–7.
67 Court of Inquiry Transcript, 9.
68 Ibid.
69 Ibid., 16.
70 Trial Transcript, 364.
71 Ibid., 212–13.

thirty feet.[72] They walked in water no higher than their knees.[73] There was mud below their feet and tall reed-like marsh grass brushing up against their legs.[74]

"Follow me," Sergeant McKeon yelled as he led the platoon along the edge of the creek. Langone stayed in the back to see that everyone entered the water.

Ervin, a recruit assigned as a right guide, went back to speak to and assist Langone in the rear. In the position of right guide, it was "his duty to march alongside McKeon...but Ervin was 'apprehensive.'"[75] Initially, Ervin was in position at the front of the column, with Wood behind him. As the platoon turned in the creek, Ervin said he went back to the point of entry in the creek to assist Langone.[76] He also had a stick in his hand, and he was swishing it in the water, saying watch out for sharks or snakes. There was a lot of kidding going on.[77] They were standing in water around the level of their hips.[78] The water never went higher than Ervin's shoulders at any time. It went slightly below his shoulder at different points when he went out, but that is as high as it ever got on him.[79]

Platoon Seventy-One continued in the creek. Column left. Column left again to form a half circle or U shape back toward the point of entry. The water was deeper then, up to their waists.[80] They remained in clusters of five to six men together, spaced fairly close to one another.[81] The joking and kidding continued as they followed Sergeant McKeon walking in the water.[82] The reed grass brushed against them, touching their ankles

---

72 Ibid., 204.

73 Ibid., 203.

74 Ibid., 203–4.

75 McKean, *Ribbon Creek*, 154.

76 Court of Inquiry Transcript, 53–57; Trial Transcript, 295–313.

77 Trial Transcript, 295–305.

78 Ibid., 298.

79 Ibid.

80 Ibid., 206.

81 Ibid.

82 Ibid., 207.

and legs.[83] The mud stuck to their feet and buried their boots up to their ankles.[84] It was not easy, as the bottom of the creek was very mucky and slimy. It caught their boots and held them in the mud. When the mud released its grasp, they slipped over the top of it. It was a rough march.[85]

Some of the men took sticks and marsh grass and waved the grass and sticks between the legs of the men in front of them and said, "Snake! Watch out—snakes!" They jiggled the grass along their feet. "Shark, shark."[86] The boys with the sticks and the jokes tried to scare some of the men marching. They succeeded in scaring their fellow recruits with marsh grass feeling to some of the men like a water moccasin slithering in the shadows. That game was going on most of the entire time.[87] It was very funny to most of them.[88] They were laughing and sloshing around the water.[89]

Sergeant McKeon yelled at them again to stop their fooling around.[90] As he marched in the mud, now waist deep in water, he was trying to teach them about combat. He warned them: "Stay close to shore. Do not go out into the middle of a waterway or a stream where you can be seen and the enemy can pick you off."[91]

There was a sliver of light reflecting on the water from a waning crescent moon that peered out from behind big black clouds above. Every now and then the moon went behind those clouds. When it came out again, Sergeant McKeon saw light on the water and told his men: "If you are ever running a problem or over in combat regarding crossing a body of water, always keep out of the light." He warned them again: "Stay in the shadows

---

83 Ibid., 221.
84 Ibid., 238.
85 Ibid., 259.
86 See note 82 above.
87 Ibid., 436–8.
88 Ibid., 246.
89 Ibid., 279.
90 Ibid., 728.
91 Ibid., 375.

and dark places close to the shore. Stay close to shore.[92] Hold your rifle above your head."[93]

He worried now that they might not stay close to shore, and so he called out two or three times: "Is everyone OK?" He heard yes.[94] He asked again, "Is anyone scared?"

One private spoke out, "Yes, sir, I'm scared."[95] It was Private Leake.

Sergeant McKeon called out: "Bring him up here."

Sergeant McKeon then left the front of the column and met Private Leake and Sygman toward the rear where they were standing in waist-deep water. Leake had slipped in the mud and gone under water. Although Leake was in a place he could stand, he was nearly paralyzed with fear. He was being supported by Sygman and Dory.[96] Sygman was carrying Leake on his back, in piggyback style, and Hartman was also assisting him up. They were in waist-deep water, no more than that.[97] Sergeant McKeon went up to them and said to Leake: "Are you scared?"

"Yes, sir."

"There is nothing to be scared of."

As he said this, Sergeant McKeon bent over and reached into the water near his thighs where marsh grass waved in and out between his legs with the flow of water. He broke off a piece of marsh grass and took it out of the water. He held the marsh grass near to Leake's face and said, "See that? There is nothing to be afraid of. It is only grass. It is just swamp grass."

Leake didn't say anything, and Sergeant McKeon saw fear in his eyes, the kind of fear that can kill a man in battle if he can't beat it. Not tonight.

---

92   Ibid., 257, 729.

93   Court of Inquiry Transcript, 33.

94   Ibid.

95   Trial Transcript, 257.

96   Ibid., 270–273.

97   Ibid.

He ordered Sygman to watch Leake.[98] Sygman then told Dory to take Leake up to the land, out of the mud.[99]

As the platoon turned left to circle back, the circle seemed to get wider. Some men began to break ranks and tread water. Treading water was easier than fighting the mud, and so they chose to tread above the mud.[100] Some did a dog paddle to avoid the mud altogether.[101] A few of the men said they wanted to swim across and began to go farther into the middle of the creek. Sergeant McKeon ordered them: "This is no swimming lesson; do not go across the creek."[102]

Sergeant McKeon headed back to the front and called out again if everyone was OK. He then called out specifically to the less-proficient swimmers. The platoon had qualified as swimmers, but some were not as good as the others. Some might be afraid like Leake, so he called out for them. Some answered, "Here." Then a cry for help came over the water.

Sergeant McKeon heard the cry for help to his rear and to his right. He was not sure at first what it was. He saw splashing. He ordered everyone out of the water, and he swam toward the commotion.[103]

The right guide was talking to Langone when he heard someone splashing. He heard a cry for help, and since there was so much joking going on, he thought it was someone fooling around.[104] Other members of the platoon also concluded it was more fooling and did not pay it much attention at first.[105] Another recruit, Carl Whitmore, did not take the cry for help seriously. He was toward the back. Alongside him was Thomas Hardeman. When they came to the tall grass along the creek, they grabbed each other's belts to avoid falling. Jerry Thomas was holding Whitmore's belt as they

---

98   Ibid., 270–80, 730.

99   Ibid., 390.

100   Court of Inquiry Transcript, 11; Trial Transcript, 378–84.

101   Court of Inquiry Transcript, 33; Trial Transcript, 378–84, 441.

102   Trial Transcript, 729.

103   Ibid., 732.

104   Ibid., 301–7.

105   Ibid., 442.

entered the water, but after entering the water, Jerry Thomas had let go of his hold on Whitmore's belt. Whitmore did not see Jerry Thomas after that.[106] Whitmore heard Sergeant McKeon ask three times if everyone was all right and heard a cry for help after the third call.

The recruits around Whitmore also heard the cry for help and said, "They are just fooling around." Someone else said, "No, they are not; they are serious." Whitmore heard several more cries for help, as well as someone calling for all good swimmers to go up front. Thomas Hardeman, a young man who wanted to be a Marine more than anything else in his life, certainly became one as he ran to the call.[107]

The first cry for help came from O'Shea.[108] O'Shea was in the third squad.[109] Jerome Daszo saw two men dive toward O'Shea.[110] Stephen McGuire had been splashing in the water, and when he heard the cry for help, he swam toward that cry. He grabbed Thompson, who was splashing for help.[111] He believed he had led Thompson to safety and left him standing in shoulder-deep water and returned to the cries for help. He wanted to take him to land, but others needed his help. He believed Thompson was safe.

Earl Grabowski swam and grabbed O'Shea. O'Shea was trying to jump on top of Grabowski, but Grabowski held him and was taking him in closer to the creek's edge. As he was bringing O'Shea in, another recruit offered help and said, "I'll take him."[112] This other recruit took O'Shea, and Grabowski went back out.

Grabowski was the only recruit to see all three recruits: Thompson, O'Shea, and Thomas Hardeman.[113] Hardeman may have been the re-

---

106 Court of Inquiry Transcript, 77.
107 Trial Transcript, 422–24.
108 Court of Inquiry Transcript, 66.
109 Ibid., 24.
110 See note 108 above.
111 Court of Inquiry Transcript, 34–36.
112 Trial Transcript, 198.
113 Ibid., 198–99.

cruit who offered to take O'Shea in. Grabowski is the only one of Platoon Seventy-One who testified under oath to having seen Hardeman after Hardeman left the seventh squad in answer to the call for good swimmers. Since Hardeman was in the vicinity of Grabowski and Grabowski was unsure whom he passed O'Shea to, it is plausible it was Hardeman. O'Shea was seen jumping on Thompson. Stephen McGuire also assisted as best he could and saw Thompson and O'Shea fighting, jumping on top of each other, and struggling.[114] McGuire said that:

> About the third time he did ask if everybody was all right, maybe fifteen seconds to a minute later, somebody yelled "help"…I looked over and everyone was just jumping, just jumping, so I started to go over there and I seen Sergeant McKeon trying to help out as best he could. Just about everybody was jumping on him there; I guess the ones that were there didn't know how to swim, some of them. Sergeant McKeon was trying to help them the best that he could; they were jumping all over him. He was trying to help them; he was trying to bring them up from the water. They were bringing him down.

McGuire thought he saw O'Shea. His statement continued:

> He had the reddest face in the platoon sir, it was just…his face was just actually like a tomato, and like I say, when I was going over to see what I could do, I seen Private Thompson and O'Shea were fighting among themselves as to who was going to stay on top of the water. They were struggling there. I got over there and I tried to help one of them and I don't know what happened to O'Shea sir, the last time I seen him sir, he was above water a little; that is the last time I seen him.[115]

---

114 Court of Inquiry Transcript, 35.
115 Ibid.

O'Shea died with the evidence on his face of this fight with Thompson. His death certificate noted a contusion over the left zygoma, more commonly known as the cheekbone.[116] He had abrasions over his right eyebrow. Accepting the sworn testimony of Grabowski and McGuire as true, Thompson and O'Shea were brought into water chest high, and O'Shea in a panic jumped over and fought with Thompson and possibly Hardeman. By the time McGuire got close enough to O'Shea, his head was slightly above water, apparently in the final stages of drowning, although McGuire did not understand what he observed. McGuire did not know what happened to O'Shea. A trained eye in rescue would have recognized the final stages of drowning, but to an untrained eye, it may have appeared deceivingly calm.

Initially an aquatic distress may be visible in a splashing. In this stage, there is a capacity to call for help. But as water enters the lungs, the final stages of drowning appear quiet and almost calm. Suffocation in water "triggers" autonomic-nervous-system responses that result in unlearned instinctive movements. Drowning victims extend their arms laterally and press down on the water's surface to keep their mouths above water, as they exhale and inhale quickly. In this stage, they have twenty to sixty seconds to live before they fall beneath the surface of the water. In its final stages, drowning is quick, and it is quiet.[117] Before O'Shea drowned, he panicked. If he was fighting with Thompson as McGuire stated, that panic spread and contributed to Thompson's death after Grabowski brought Thompson to where he could stand. Thompson's vulnerability may have been due to his struggle in the water and his fear. Thompson and O'Shea both drowned that night.

The panic spread beyond O'Shea and Thompson. Immediately after the cries for help, Thomas was walking with Geckle and Poole. There were two squads still behind them.[118] As they walked in the mud, none of the

---

116 Trial Transcript, Prosecution Exhibit Sixteen.

117 Mario Vittone and Francesco Pia, "It Doesn't Look Like They're Drowning: How to Recognize the Instinctive Drowning Response," *On Scene* (Fall 2006): 14.

118 Trial Transcript, 431–32.

three were good swimmers, so they held on to one another as best they could. The water never rose above the chest pocket of Geckle, who stood at five feet eight inches, except once when he slipped. He slipped and went under water holding Jerry Thomas. Jerry Thomas was five feet six and half inches and weighed 120 pounds. He was seventeen years and four months old. Geckle held Thomas, and Poole held Geckle, as they walked in the mud. Poole let go of Geckle, and Geckle slipped under the water. Thomas pulled Geckle under the water two times. Geckle broke away from Thomas under the water and dug himself out to shallower water.[119] When he came up out of the water, he did not see Thomas.[120]

Ervin saw Wood from where he'd gone to see Langone. Private Wood had his hands above his head, perhaps attempting to learn how to hold a rifle in water. The water appeared to be up to his chest. Wood was talking to another person. The mud was slippery. Wood was tall, and other people held on to his shoulders to get their balance. Wood was trying to keep his own balance, and he told the men jumping on him: "Get off my shoulders." He appeared to Ervin "as if he was standing but there were men hanging on him, seemed to be pulling him down."[121] Wood was six feet one inches tall, weighed 173 pounds, and was seventeen years and ten months old. He came from New York.[122] Wood began to panic as other men pulled him down into the water.

Everyone got scared as pockets of panic broke out among them.[123] Richard Acker was walking next to Charles Reilly toward the rear of the column when the panic first started. It felt as though a current pulled them out. Reilly got scared and grabbed hold of Acker, hanging on to his belt and collar. Reilly was trying to keep himself up by pulling Acker under the water. Acker tried to help him, but it became too much for him. Reilly was

---

119 Court of Inquiry Transcript, 83.
120 Trial Transcript, 431–33.
121 Court of Inquiry Transcript, 57.
122 Trial Transcript, Prosecution Exhibit Sixteen.
123 Court of Inquiry Transcript, 51.

drowning Acker, and Acker had to break away. When Acker broke away from Reilly, that was the last he saw of him.[124]

Private Brewer swam toward the commotion and helped someone into the edge of the creek. He headed back to help more. He saw Wood and cupped his hand under Wood's chin. Wood panicked and climbed on top of Brewer. He carried Brewer under, and after he had him under water, he grabbed his legs. Brewer pulled away and did not see him after that.[125]

Martinez saw Wood and tried to help him. He said:

He was a few feet away from me. When I got to him, he was practically finished already. He had so much water in his lungs he couldn't cry for help. All I heard was like when you gargle your throat. There was water in his lungs sir. I latched onto him and started pulling him in. He grabbed the cord around my neck, sir, and he pulled me down and I went down once. I had to let go and he came back up with me and I grabbed onto him again and some of the boys that were drowning right next to him grabbed onto me also and I had to push him away and they took me down again. I had to let go of Private Wood sir. I couldn't hold on because I had my boots on and all my clothes and I was going down. I don't think I would have come up if I went down again.[126]

Sergeant McKeon heard the splashing and cries for help. He was leading the platoon in the front, and the cry came from his right and behind him as he was headed back to the point of entry. The sound was farther out than he was. He started swimming toward this area where he heard the sound of splashing and the cry for help. There was a kid who looked like he was going the wrong way; he had his back toward Sergeant McKeon. Sergeant McKeon pulled him in about ten feet toward the creek's edge. He was

---

124 Ibid., 72.
125 Ibid., 42.
126 Ibid., 68.

assured the kid could stand and was OK, so he headed back out to where he saw splashing. He saw Wood, who appeared to be calm and coming in. McKeon ignored him because he did not appear to be in distress. McKeon intended to go farther out to the few more beyond Wood he saw splashing. He thought Wood was going to be all right. Then Wood latched onto him, grabbed his neck, and surprised him. McKeon tried to break the hold, as he was treading water. Wood grabbed him and brought him down. When they came up, McKeon screamed at him, "Keep your head, and I'll get you in." Wood wasn't saying anything, not a thing. They went down a second time, and it seemed to McKeon that Wood pulled him down deeper than the first time. All McKeon could think of was to get to the top. He was pulling toward the top, and Wood let go, the kid let go.[127]

Sergeant McKeon came up gasping for air, looking all around him in the water. He did not see anyone, so he swam around searching. He dove beneath the surface and opened his arms into the water, reaching for Wood. Water flowed through his fingers and in his eyes. There was nothing there but water. He came up for air. He knew that he had lost him. He had lost Wood, maybe more. He said, "Oh my God, what have I done?"

The now-silenced cries for help pierced through the platoon, and the panic it brought drowned the lives of six recruits: Norman Alfred Wood, Jerry Lamonte Thomas, Donald Francis O'Shea, Leroy Thompson, Charles Francis Reilly, and another who was the only one among the dead who was a strong swimmer and who ran to their rescue, Thomas Curtis Hardeman.

The magnitude of the exercise gone wrong weighed more heavily with each stroke Sergeant McKeon took toward the creek's edge. When he got to the edge, he could barely stand and was helped out of the water by two recruits. All the recruits said McKeon was the last one out of the water. Martinez wanted to go to look for the lost recruits, but Moran was afraid more would drown and did not want Martinez to go back in the water. Moran lied to Martinez and said, "Everybody is OK." Martinez did not

---

127 Trial Transcript, 732.

hear any more splashes or cries for help. He recalled, "For some reason it was hard to believe but I believed it and I swam in."[128]

Private Maloof walked next to Sergeant McKeon away from the creek that had swallowed his men. Maloof asked Sergeant McKeon, "Sir, do you need any help?"

"No."

"Are you sure, sir?"

Sergeant McKeon mumbled, "We lost a lot of men in there."

"Yes, sir. Shall we go back and get them?"

"No, we will never find them; there is not enough light."[129]

Sergeant McKeon was afraid more lives would be lost if they looked for them. They were gone.

Sergeant McKeon walked ahead to Whitmore, who was helping Leake. He asked Whitmore where he was taking him.

Whitmore answered, "The barracks."

Sergeant McKeon said, "Take him to sick bay," and as he did, Whitmore saw the sadness on Sergeant McKeon's face.[130] It was a haunting sadness that would spread out from the young men of Platoon Seventy-One to the heart of the Marine Corps.

Moran also walked closely by Sergeant McKeon as they left Ribbon Creek. Moran recalled that Sergeant McKeon "was pretty shook up, sir. He was…I don't know…he wasn't…he was in a state of shock more or less. He was talking about the men out there, we left men out there, just more or less talking to himself sir. And I asked him if he wanted a cigarette and he said no and he didn't seem to be paying much attention or where he was either."[131]

Sergeant McKeon was mumbling to himself in shock and disbelief. His only thought was for the men in his command, some of them now lost. It was between 8:45 p.m. and 9:00 p.m.[132]

---

128 Court of Inquiry Transcript, 70.
129 Trial Transcript, 267.
130 Ibid., 422–27.
131 Court of Inquiry Transcript, 12.
132 Ibid., 107.

The corporal at the guard at Parris Island heard the yelling behind the butts and called Technical Sergeant John Taylor to tell him of the noise. In response to hearing the report of yelling behind the butts, Sergeant Taylor got in his car and drove down to the area. When he first arrived, he could not see anything. He cut the motor and listened. He heard the yelling farther off and got back in his car and drove down closer to the creek and behind Charlie Butts. He listened again. He still heard noise coming from the area of the creek, but he could not see anything in the dark. He turned his car around from a position that was vertically parallel to the creek and pointed the headlights directly toward Ribbon Creek. He then began walking toward the creek. He saw boys coming out of the water of the creek. Two boys, Sygman and Whitmore, were slowly coming from the far right side of where the other boys were coming out of the water. Sygman and Whitmore were carrying Leake.

Sergeant Taylor yelled out to them, "What is going on?"

They ignored him and refused to say anything.[133] Sergeant Taylor heard someone in the distance near the creek yell, "The lights are blinding us! Cut the lights!"

Sergeant Taylor ran back to his car and cut the lights. The boys of Platoon Seventy-One were passing him now, some nearly naked, some without shoes, all wet, all cold.

He asked frantically, "Where is the drill instructor?"

No one answered him. The majority of the platoon had passed him when he first saw Sergeant McKeon.

He demanded of Sergeant McKeon, "What the hell is going on?"

Sergeant McKeon saw that Sergeant Taylor had a duty belt on and, because of it, recognized Sergeant Taylor to have a position of authority. Sergeant McKeon looked directly at Sergeant Taylor and answered, "I'm responsible for this."[134]

Sergeant Taylor asked, "Well, are you missing any men?"

---

133 Ibid., 108.
134 Ibid.; Trial Transcript, 733.

"There may be three."[135]

Sergeant Taylor said, "Get a count on your men, and get back to your barracks as quickly as you can. And I will meet you up there." He then told the two boys slowly making their way holding Leake to get in his car and he would drive them to sick bay.

On the way to sick bay, he stopped at the Charlie ammunition shed located on the road between the Baker and Charlie Ranges. The ammunition shed had a phone located in "a little cubbyhole inside the bulkhead there."[136] He needed to get help. There was no light to see the phone, so he took out a cigarette lighter from his pocket and dialed the corporal of the guard, weapons battalion, and said, "Get the captain of the day, and get him over to Charlie Butts on the double. We have trouble down here. We have a platoon coming from Ribbon Creek, some possibly lost."

He wanted to call Colonel McKean, but his cigarette lighter ran out of fluid.[137]

Captain Patrick was the officer of the day at the weapons training battalion. He was watching the Sunday night movie when he was called to the phone. He took the call from the corporal of the guard. Captain Patrick "hastened to the scene." It was 9:00 p.m.[138]

Captain Patrick arrived at the Charlie ammunition shed. Sergeant Taylor was headed to his car so that he could face the headlights toward the cubbyhole where the phone was located when Patrick drove up to him. Patrick saw Platoon Seventy-One passing him in bunches; a few of them were being carried. They looked bedraggled to him: wet, muddy, and in varying states of undress. He asked Sergeant Taylor what happened. Sergeant Taylor told him that he had seen the platoon leaving the water's edge and then relayed that the drill sergeant involved, Sergeant McKeon, told him that a man had jumped on Sergeant McKeon's back in the water

---

135 Trial Transcript, 189.

136 Ibid.

137 Ibid.

138 Ibid., 185; Court of Inquiry Transcript, 108.

and then the section leader disappeared.[139] Sergeant McKeon thought some were lost.

Sergeant Taylor said to Captain Patrick, "I told the DI to get a count on the men and meet me in the barracks."[140]

As he said this, Sergeant McKeon came up to Captain Patrick, who then asked him: "Are all the men out of the water? Is there anyone left down there?"

"There might be three or four left down in the water."[141]

Captain Patrick's instructions to Sergeant McKeon were the same as Taylor's, to get a count and get back to barracks.

As Captain Patrick spoke to Sergeant McKeon, Sergeant Taylor turned his car toward the bulkhead where the phone was situated. He then went up to the phone and began dialing Colonel McKean. As Colonel McKean's phone rang, Taylor handed the phone to Captain Patrick who had just walked in.[142] McKean testified to the conversation as follows:

" 'Colonel, this is Patrick. We're in trouble. There are a bunch of recruits coming back to building 761 and it seems that the DI has been marching them through the swamps. I'm going now to investigate it.' I said to Patrick, "Lock up the DI. Send to sick bay those that need it. Get the rest of them policed up and call me back as soon as you know the number of that platoon and the battalion.' "[143]

Anne's younger brother, Sgt. Matthew McKeon, was arrested that night on the foregoing order of Colonel McKean. M. P. Fred MaGruder took him into custody almost as soon as he arrived at the barracks. Doctors examined him. An investigator took a statement. Within less than twenty-four hours and by the evening of April 9, 1956, the commandant of the Marine Corps, General Pate, made a public statement to the press that

---

139 McKean, *Ribbon Creek*, 22.

140   Court of Inquiry Transcript, 108.

141   Trial Transcript, 186.

142   Ibid., 189.

143   Court of Inquiry Transcript, 222.

effectively "accused McKeon of manslaughter" before the court of inquiry even convened.[144]

The quick and decisive strategy of "locking up the DI" and quickly convicting him of manslaughter might have worked more smoothly if it were not for Anne, myself, and a few good lawyers from New York.

144 Keith Fleming, *U.S. Marine Corps in Crisis* (Columbia: University of South Carolina Press, 1990), 44.

CHAPTER TWO

––––

AT 10:00 P.M. ON APRIL 13, 1956, I and a colleague, Jim McGarry, boarded a train to Yemassee, South Carolina, from New York's Pennsylvania Station, the old Penn Station back before they tore it down. We rushed beneath Penn Station's imposing concourse of steel and glass that mirrored a blue luminous New York sky above us. We descended stairs with rails of oak and wrought iron to board the Silver Meteor South for Yemassee, South Carolina. Our destination was the southeast-coast training depot for United States Marine Corps, Parris Island, South Carolina, where my brother-in-law S. Sgt. Matthew McKeon was in the middle of a court of inquiry. The court of inquiry had been commenced on April 10, 1956, pursuant to the order of the commanding general assigned to Parris Island, United States Marine Corps General Burger.

Jim and I were members of the Bar in the State of New York, both graduates of Fordham University School of Law (I from the class of 1952). The investigation by the court of inquiry that was appointed by General Burger was akin to a grand-jury proceeding. Criminal charges were likely to result, even though we hoped otherwise. Two days of testimony had already been taken. We were late. The inquiry panel had stopped midway in the proceedings and was waiting for us, Sergeant McKeon's civilian counsel, to arrive.

We rode the train through every city along the East Coast from New York to South Carolina, passing familiar cities such as Newark, New

Jersey; Trenton, New Jersey; Washington, DC; and Baltimore, Maryland. Then we headed into the deeper south wherein the sky grew darker, and the names of the cities became less familiar and sounded strange, such as Florence, South Carolina, and finally Yemassee. I disliked traveling then, and I like it even less now. Trains and travel have always reminded me of World War II and of farewells: some that were final, and others that were not. I never knew which it would be. I still don't.

In 1942, it was the number-six train to Penn Station that took me from home to Georgetown in my freshman year. In that same year, World War II interrupted college for travels to military bases and to unforgotten worlds abroad. In June of 1943, I traveled to Fort Dix, New Jersey, and soon after to Camp Wheeler in Macon, Georgia, to complete my basic training. On December 17, 1943, I headed home from basic training on a delayed train route that took ten days until finally I reached Pelham Bay Station. My younger brother Joe returned home the following day, also on a delayed route. We knew what that meant. It meant overseas duty for both of us. I was home for eight days, scheduled to report to Camp Patrick Henry on January 6, 1944.

In January 1944, my final destination in combat was the American landing in Anzio, Italy. In Anzio, I was captured by the Germans and taken from Italy to a prison camp in Germany where I stayed for a year. At night sometimes I still hear the sound of German soldiers yelling in my darker dreams, yelling the sound of death in German. When I wake up now, I think that after prison in Germany, there is nothing to be afraid of.

The voice of the Nazis yelling was the last thing I heard before they took me prisoner. They would have killed me if it were not for Bernie (Ziegfried Bernheim). Bernie was a German Jewish ex-patriot from a distinguished wealthy family in Germany who had fled Berlin before the Nazis took control. Then he joined the American forces and went back to Germany.

Bernie kept our spirits high with jokes that poked fun at the army for the grub they served us. He was with me on the ship to Anzio and with me in the foxhole the night I was captured. I had been sleeping: on break from keeping watch but ready in rest with one hand on a grenade as I slept upright against the dirt and wood of our foxhole. I heard German commands in my sleep. I saw German soldiers standing above the foxhole. I was ready to throw the grenade until I saw Bernie sitting across from me in the foxhole. He mouthed the words, "Give it up, Tom. It is useless. We are surrounded." The foxholes that had had Americans in them before I slept were all empty with surrender.

I think of Bernie often. I still wonder exactly what happened to him, though I think I know. There is a book I received as a gift that lists all the American troops in World War II. I found Bernie's name, and they have him listed as missing in action with a cross next to his name. But I was with him when we were both captured, so he was not missing in action as recorded. I think the Nazis found out he was a German Jew, and they must have killed him right there for being Jewish. They shot him, I am sure. He was not correctly recorded as a prisoner. He wasn't missing in action. He was murdered. I wish I could correct that record.

Those nights of death return often, and as I rode on the train to Yemassee to another base, I thought of how close I came to not making it back home. Now there were six more young men who would not return home. They were about the same age I was at nineteen in that foxhole.

I also thought of the week that brought me yet again heading toward an American military-training depot. My week had started on Monday, April 9, 1956, in the New York County Courthouse where I took my first defense verdict for A&P Crane Rental and its insurance carrier. Many such verdicts would follow in my life, but that was my first real trial success. I had spent late nights researching case law and preparing my direct and cross-examinations, and between weekend chores, I prayed. Anne and I had our faith and our prayers in common. I am not really sure who the good Lord listened to, me or Anne, but it was probably Anne.

On Monday morning, April 9, I appeared in the New York County Courthouse ready to argue a motion to dismiss, which was handily denied by the presiding judge. That day I gave my first real closing argument in a case that went to a jury and came back with a verdict for my client and against the plaintiff. The plaintiff was represented by Harry Zeitlan. Zeitlan, who in 1956 was a big-shot New York City negligence lawyer—which I was not quite yet but hoped I would become. I was no Zeitlan with a house in the Hamptons, but I was always prepared in a courtroom. Preparation is the key to trial work. I knew if I could outprepare any opponent, I had a chance against anyone. I was pretty successful with that formula, except for the house in the Hamptons that I never bought, which was all right by me. I am happy where I have lived for more than fifty years in my house on City Island, a little mile-and-a-half-long island in the most northeastern section of New York City. It is surrounded by Eastchester Bay on one side and the Long Island Sound on the other.

I celebrated my defense victory with a toast in Pelham Bay Tavern as I waited for Anne to pick me up at the station. That night, as Anne and I listened to the evening news, a report came over the television that six Marines had died in a swamp march in Parris Island on Sunday night and a seventh recruit was missing. The news anchor also reported that General Pate, commandant of the United States Marine Corps, was on the scene at Parris Island at a news conference held at approximately 5:00 p.m. on Monday evening, during which General Pate reported that it appeared the drill staff sergeant who had conducted the march broke regulations. An official court of inquiry would convene on Tuesday, April 10, 1956, to consider appropriate charges, including homicide and oppression of troops. The Marine sergeant was married with two children. They offered no other details, they gave no names, but Anne instinctively knew it was Matty and said so the minute she heard the report. By morning, we knew she was right.

On Tuesday morning, April 10, 1956, my brother-in-law S. Sgt. Matthew McKeon appeared in every headline of every newspaper in the country. The *New York Times* headline read as follows: "Five Marines Die in Swamp in Parris Island March; Another Recruit Missing—General Pate at Scene for Personal Inquiry."[145] The *Boston Globe* brought the news to Matt's hometown, reporting that a Worcester Marine sergeant was in custody last night pending a probe after five drown on hike.[146] Every newscast during the day quoted Matt or spoke of him.

Matt had led his platoon on a night march in a swampy creek on Parris Island on Sunday night. Six men had drowned. General Pate's public announcement at the news conference on Monday evening that Sergeant McKeon broke regulations as well the immediate commencement of a court of inquiry led us to believe that the Marine Corps intended to throw the book at Matt and absolve itself of any wrongdoing. Anne and I never saw it any other way.

Anne's plan to help Matt was to get me to Parris Island as soon as possible. Her brother Matt, who was closest in age to her, had served in the navy in World War II. In fact, almost her entire family had served, including Anne herself. Anne actually outranked me in the army as a sergeant, because all nurses were officers and I was just a private. As her brothers fought and saw combat, she saw and nursed the wounds of combat. All of us had World War II in our shared consciousness. We all served, and we all made it home. Giving up was not in our vocabulary. None of us were going to give Matt up for anything or to anybody, not even the Marine Corps. His past service had been exemplary, but even if it hadn't, we would not have done anything differently. His years of service were not in the forefront in those days, but the war experience had influenced his decisions in training.

Matt joined the navy at age seventeen and was assigned to the commissioned carrier, USS *Essex*. Brigadier General McKean in his memoir, *Ribbon Creek,* includes proud homage to that ship. His deep pride at the service of *Essex* bears including some battle facts he mentioned. The *Essex* was deservedly beloved and historically significant, as it was instrumental in the US victory and Japan's defeat in World War II. It engaged in eighty-seven actions that included attacks on the Marcus Islands, Rabaul, Tarawa,

---

145 *New York Times*, April 10, 1956.
146 *Boston Globe*, April 10, 1956.

Truk, Saipan, Pescadores, Formosa, Saigon, Hong Kong, Kure, Kwajalein, and Hokkaido, and supporting combat operations in Bougainville, Rabaul, the Gilberts, Marshalls, Mariannas, Iwo Jima, and Okinawa.[147] It participated in the battles in the Philippines Sea and assisted in the attack of Yamoto that ended "effective power of the Japanese surface navy. *Essex* destroyed 1,531 enemy aircraft and probably destroyed another 800; she sank or damaged 419 ships."[148] The *Essex* survived a kamikaze hit, a typhoon, and World War II with Matt McKeon on her guns, fighting and surviving on the sea fortress. The statistics tell as much about the ship as they do about the men on it.

Less than two years after Matt's honorable discharge from service in World War II, he reenlisted with the US Marines in May of 1948.[149] He taught combat tactics at Quantico and reenlisted again in 1952. The night of April 8, 1956, Matt thought he was teaching his platoon combat tactics and discipline. Matt was just their age when he first entered the service at seventeen. At age thirty-two, fifteen years after enlisting and serving proudly, Matt was confined in the brig on Parris Island, awaiting the court-of-inquiry conclusion, which would surely result in a full court-martial.

The commanders of the US Marines could say what they would, but Anne believed in Matt unconditionally, and her service in the army left her fearless to say so and to take action to defend her family. She was also fearless when it came to telling me what to do. Matt's criminal defense started in earnest with his sister Anne. Anne was convinced that Matt was not going to get a fair trial without my intervention. She was relentless in her efforts to convince me. But I had cases on the New York county-trial calendar Thursday morning. I could not just leave New York—maybe by Thursday after I appeared in court and only then if the cases were continued to another date. I told Anne that, but the way she persisted in telling

147 Trial Transcript, 679.

148 McKean, *Ribbon Creek*, 431.

149 Trial Transcript, 681.

me to get to Parris Island to represent Matt, I knew that if I did not go, our marriage would be over.

By Tuesday night, Anne had her family in Worcester convinced that Matt's appointed lawyer was not enough alone. After she spoke with family in Worcester, the McKeon family at Anne's urging decided that I would represent Matt. I would like to say in retrospect that it was my idea, but it was not. I had no choice at all.

The next morning, Anne and I waited at Grand Central Station for Anne's parents, Jim and Alice McKeon, to arrive in New York from Worcester. They had intended to spend the night in New York and then go on to South Carolina. We waited until the train from Boston arrived, but there was no sign of them. Rather than take a train, they had decided to drive directly to Parris Island from Worcester. Anne's brothers Jimmy, Ned, and Francis, and her sister, Ellen, were all headed to Parris Island, South Carolina, by car. It was at least a twenty-hour drive from Massachusetts.

As Anne and I drove home from Grand Central on the FDR North to the Bruckner Expressway toward City Island, we listened to news reports on the radio about the ongoing court of inquiry. A psychiatrist had testified about Matt's mental condition. We were infuriated when we heard that he was even examined by a psychiatrist. Anne thought they wanted to throw Matt in the slammer and say he was crazy. Her instincts were not without support in the news reports.

On Wednesday, April 11, the Associated Press submitted a report to the *New York Times* that was published on April 12. This report echoed the radio reports we heard the day before. The headlines read as follows: "Marine Sergeant Gets Mental Test." The news article reported that the psychiatric examination of Matt was ordered on Monday by General Burger, who appeared at a press conference during the break in the inquiry proceedings that day. He announced that the psychiatric examination was performed by Lt. Charles Herlihy. The press asked General Burger if there was any reason to suppose that Sergeant McKeon had been drinking or had become emotionally unbalanced before ordering his platoon on the march, to which General Burger replied, "I just can't answer; I just don't know."[150]

When Anne heard that report on the radio, her fearlessness tripped over the terror of what might result from such an exam. I knew then she was right. I had to go as soon as possible. I told Anne to book a Thursday night train if possible and not to wait until Friday. It was a gamble that I could get out of my scheduled trial in New York, but it seemed the only thing to do. It calmed Anne down a little.

She asked, "What are we going to do, Tom?"

I said, "You are going to book me on a train to Yemassee for Thursday night, and I am going to Parris Island. And we are going to fight."

Fight. I think now of the fight of trials, of wars, of the fight to get that Thursday morning trial in New York adjourned so I could go to Yemassee, and of the fights we had. How splendidly Anne and I could fight. The fight in Anne was something to love, something I loved. I am pretty sure it probably saved Matt from jail and it sure as hell saved me some twenty years later when drinking became less of a leisurely social activity than a habit of the heart and an inhabitant of the soul. Anne could fight.

On Thursday morning, Anne McKeon Costello introduced herself to the Marine Corps via long-distance telephone and ordered them to stop the inquiry until Sergeant McKeon's lawyer, yours truly, Thomas P. Costello, arrived in South Carolina. She told them not to speak to Matt and not to exam him anymore outside the presence of his attorney. The Marine Corps could just wait until defense counsel got there, and she gave them my office number. The Marine Corps followed the instructions of now-retired Army Sergeant Anne McKeon. The inquiry stopped, and the assigned defense counsel called me or tried to, but I was unreachable by phone in the New York County Courthouse.

As Anne ordered the United States Marine Corps to stop the inquiry from her phone in City Island, I was in Manhattan rushing up the long shallow steps leading to the New York County Supreme Court. The low

---

150 *New York Times*, April 12, 1956.

depth of the steps seemed designed for a contemplative pace that was an unwanted luxury that morning. I skipped every other step and entered the court at 9:20 a.m. for a 9:30 a.m. calendar call.

The daily business of the New York County's trial part could be seen and heard in the courtroom that morning, as lawyers reviewed files sitting in the hard wooden benches of the courtroom and other lawyers spoke in low hurried tones to broker a last-minute settlement before jury selection. I joined them, anxious to get my case adjourned, which in New York practice means continued to another date. My purpose was to get to Parris Island.

The presiding judge over New York County's trial part on April 12, 1956, was the Honorable Judge McGivern. Judge McGivern was the son of an iceman who with the support of Tammany Hall became the presiding justice of the appellate division.[151] Judge McGivern had not yet risen to the appellate division in April 1956, although I wish he had. He was then presiding over the trial part in Manhattan with a particular plague of unreasonableness that reigns over many a courtroom in and beyond New York that has at its root an unspoken yet familiar theme in politics and government of: who do you think you are and what can you do or have you done for me lately?

The calendar was called timely at 9:30 a.m. Judge McGivern took the bench as the court officer announced, "All rise." The lawyers rose to their feet. The judge then sat, and the lawyers followed in the silent "Simon Says"-like gestures of respect that are adhered to in every courtroom to this day. The chatting quieted to an occasional rush of paper until only the voices of the lawyers answering the call could be heard. The plaintiff was always ready. Defense? Rarely ready. There is in civil-defense work sometimes a sense of delay commonly referred to as "delay, delay, delay," which is preceded only by "deny, deny, deny." Maybe that shopworn response is all McGivern heard when I answered the call of the calendar and said: "I have been retained by S. Sgt. Matt McKeon to assist in his defense of

---

151 *New York Times Obituary*, 1998.

court-of-inquiry proceedings in Parris Island. The proceedings have already commenced, and I need to travel tonight to attend the proceedings and respectfully request an adjournment."

The judge responded, "Denied."

I was stunned and heartbroken. I had promised Matt and promised Anne I would get to Parris Island. Luckily, or politically, my boss, Whelan, intervened and called McGivern later that morning and got the case put over.

At the same time Judge McGivern was denying my request in New York, Lieutenant Collins, Matt's assigned counsel on Parris Island, was requesting a continuance of the court of inquiry pending my arrival, but he reported to the court that he was unable to actually reach me that morning. All in all, he had an easier time of it in front of seasoned Marine Corps officers presiding over the inquiry, who granted a continuance until Saturday, than I'd had in New York that morning.

By the time I returned to the office Thursday morning, I had several phone messages from Lieutenant Collins. I did not get back to him with my final travel plans until Thursday afternoon because the plans were too fluid to confirm until McGivern changed his denial to "granted." When finally I gave Lieutenant Collins my travel itinerary, he generously offered to meet Jim McGarry and me at Yemassee Station. I learned that the court of inquiry would resume on Saturday morning, which gave me just a day to get there and less than that to prepare.

On the way home that Thursday afternoon, I stopped by my alma mater, Fordham Law, then located at 302 Broadway, right down the block from my office, which was also on Broadway. I asked for help from my former professor, Assistant Dean William Hughes Mulligan. I needed insight for strategy and maybe the assistance of Fordham's legal network. If charges resulted from the court of inquiry, I could not try this case alone. Dean Mulligan would know where to start. After I left Fordham that day, I suspect Dean Mulligan may have made even more calls than I know of.

From Fordham Law on Broadway, I went to the Wall Street Station and caught the 4/5 express train to 125th Street and then switched to the number 6 to Pelham Bay in the Bronx. Anne was waiting for me at Pelham Bay Station, and we drove back to City Island where a hot dinner waited and a packed suitcase of white, starched shirts, my two best suits, and newly shined shoes. As I ate dinner, Anne packed my briefcase with several new legal pads and pens. There was no detail she overlooked. After dinner Anne drove me to Pennsylvania Station where I met Jim McGarry and we boarded the Silver Meteor. We unloaded our bags in the car and had a long-awaited nightcap together before the long night's ride.

By Friday morning when I awoke, the train had crossed the Mason Dixon line with several hours left until we reached Yemassee. I dressed and went to the dining car for coffee and the morning papers. The papers were full of the Parris Island story again, as well as the progress of the inquiry proceedings. Jim McGarry was reading the *New York Times.* He folded the paper as I joined him and said that the *Times* reported that General Pate said that a psychiatric examination of Sergeant McKeon showed a perfectly sound, well-balanced young man who was sound when he did it and sound now. McKeon exhibited proper and appropriate remorse. The psychiatrist concluded that Sergeant McKeon "made an error in judgment," to which General Pate commented that this was just one man's opinion. I was infuriated.

I looked up from the paper and asked Jim: "Now why did Pate have to add that comment: 'it is just one man's opinion.'"

Jim offered, "It diminishes his opinion, it is dismissive of it, and it doesn't support a criminal theory."

I said, "It makes out an accident. That is why 'an error in judgment, simple negligence, not murder.'"

Jim looked up from his folded paper and said, "Covering themselves… that is their job, I guess."

I could only think of our job ahead: catching up on the proceedings and reviewing them. I could not think of their job. I said, "And we will have a job reading those transcripts before we start. They took several witnesses already."

I started feeling a little low then, wondering if we could get all the work we needed to get done before Saturday.

Jim responded, "The fact that they took so many witnesses only hurts us to the extent that we have to read the testimony and could not be there to assess it. But otherwise I don't think that it's so bad because they took the privates or 'boots,' I guess they call them. Not much you could do with them, Tom. They are like the elderly or children—you can't touch them on the stand, or you look like a heel."

It was an excellent point Jim made. We planned what strategy we could that morning with the limited information we had. We would agree with the psychiatrist. It was an error in judgment or, more simply put, an accident. The second point of our defense strategy was to show that night marches such as the one conducted on April 8, 1956, were part of Parris Island practice. We hoped to prove those two points and mitigate criminal intent.

As I continued reading about the case in the papers, a court-martial seemed more certain with every word. General Burger, commanding officer at Parris Island, was quoted as saying a swamp march took place in 1954 wherein the sergeant drew a court-martial as a result. Generals Pate and Burger were not leaving much room for anything but a court-martial.

Details of masses, coffins, and funeral arrangements filled the remainder of the coverage. On Friday, Lt. Cdr. Anthony Bielski sang a requiem high mass at Parris Island for O'Shea. Just six days earlier, Father Bielski had given Donald O'Shea communion. A photograph was taken from the back of the church filled with Marines in attendance. Their backs were straight, and their shoulders were square and rigid against the pews of the church as though at attention. Additional Protestant services were held for the remaining five recruits who lost their lives, after which a funeral plane left Parris Island carrying some of their coffins that were flown north to

New York's International Airport in Queens, where three coffins were removed from the plane and a fourth went on to Syracuse.

More articles and more photographs filled every paper. There were photographs of coffins draped in the flag of the United States. One photograph that took up half a page in the *Times* depicted Donald O'Shea's coffin being carried by six Marines as another stood guard next to the plane that had flown Donald O'Shea and four others home to New York. The photo overshadowed the entire page, with the names of the dead below: Donald Francis O'Shea, Bleecker Street, Brooklyn, New York; Charles Francis Reilly, 18, Clyde, New York; Leroy Thompson, 18, 296 Quincey Street, Brooklyn; Norman Alfred Wood, 17, Dowsing Street, Brooklyn; and Jerry Lamont Thomas, Alexandria, Virginia. The sixth, Curtis Thomas Hardeman, was taken on a separate plane to Vidalia, Georgia. They were boys, just boys like we were when we were enlisted and drafted into World War II, like I was on the train to Camp Patrick Henry, except I was able to say good-bye.

The papers would be filled with the news and photos of the tragedy at Ribbon Creek for weeks. The coverage was nonstop until as Anne later recalled: "Only the sinking of the *Andrea Doria* in July of that year took Matt out of the headlines."

At three o'clock on Friday, April 13, 1956, we arrived at Yemassee Station, South Carolina. Lt. Jeremiah Collins met us as promised. Lieutenant Collins was tall with thick black hair framing his face. His face rounded with a smile as he greeted us, and it was clear he was much younger than us. Lieutenant Collins briefed us on the hearing as we drove to Parris Island.

The inquiry started on the morning of April 10 with a scene inspection. Sergeant McKeon did not want to go, and Lieutenant Collins stayed back with him. Looking back at it, it would have been helpful if there were more lawyers at the time so a defense presence could have been at the scene inspection with the judges, but there was no defense attorney present. This gave the prosecution an opportunity to elicit unchallenged testimony concerning location from two Marines who did not arrive until after the incident or, put another way, could offer only speculation as to the exact location. Matt could have used more than one lawyer from the start, but then again, in fairness to the Corps, the Corps had to persuade Matt to accept any counsel in the very beginning.

Matt's remorse paralyzed him at first. He did not want a lawyer. He did not want a trial. He just wanted to accept responsibility. But the nature of the responsibility was not clear to anyone at first, least of all to Matt. In stark juxtaposition to Matt's personal remorse and guilt was the Marines' lack of any. The Marine Corps appeared at first to distance itself from Matt and from any culpability. Both Matt's remorse and the Marines' rush from any would prove to be equally misguided.

General Burger ordered the inquiry on Monday morning and testimony began on Tuesday. General Burger appointed a three-member board of inquiry consisting of two majors and a lieutenant. The inquiry opened with the standard procedure of advising Sergeant McKeon of his rights. The appointing order and authority of the panel was read in open court. There was no objection to any member of the court. General Burger's order directing the commencement of the court of inquiry drew attention to Section 0304 of the Naval Supplement for Court Martials, allowing for additional parties to be charged. In short, anyone who testified could be targeted and included in the criminal investigation. The not-so-veiled threat of criminal charges was a ploy played through the court-martial to limit testimony of the practice of past night marches. It did not entirely work because many witnesses were, after all, Marines. Several Marines who testified at the court-martial proved undaunted in the face of express warnings of potential culpability emanating from the prosecution. But at the time of the inquiry, while no witness took the Fifth, most witnesses were more guarded.

Counsel for the court, or in the vernacular, the prosecuting attorney, was Major Holben. At 9:00 a.m. on Tuesday, April 10, 1956, the members of the court and Major Holben viewed the area of Ribbon Creek behind

Charlie Butts in the general location where the incident occurred. Two guides, Major Stanley McLeod and Staff Sergeant Sparks, were present at the scene. General Burger's appointment of officers to the inquiry panel of rank no higher than the lieutenant proved problematic when Colonel McKean was scheduled to testify. McKean was the colonel in charge of weapons battalion, the number-two man on Parris Island after Major General Burger. General Burger issued a curative second order on the morning of April 13, 1956, after the president of the court, Colonel Heles, announced that they might need testimony from Colonel McKean because the incident occurred behind weapons battalion. Given the seniority issues, the members of the court could not question McKean. General Burger conveyed the problem to General Pate. General Pate offered Brigadier General Greene. General Burger immediately issued an order appointing Brig. Gen. Wallace Greene as a senior member of the court of inquiry. General Burger would not be taking the stand, just McKean.[152]

One hundred and fifty-four legal-size pages of inquiry testimony represented the testimony of twenty-two recruits taken on Tuesday, Wednesday, and part of Thursday until Anne managed to pause the proceedings with her phone call. I asked about the psychiatric exam. We learned that Sergeant McKeon was examined on April 9 by Lt. Charles Herlihy, Medical Corps, US Navy. He had testified the day before our arrival, taking the stand at approximately 8:00 a.m. He was the psychiatrist in charge of the depot and had been requested to examine McKeon by the chief of staff of the US Marine Corps Depot, Parris Island. He performed a neuropsychiatric exam because of certain medical complaints Sergeant McKeon offered during the exam. Sergeant McKeon's back had been bothering him for over a month, and as a matter of fact, he had been limping. We would have to review the transcript and prepare for the testimony of Dr. Atcheson, who administered the Bogen's test of alcohol, and Colonel McKean.

---

152 McKean, *Ribbon Creek*, 506; Fleming, *U.S. Marine Corps in Crisis*, 50; Court of Inquiry Transcript, Exhibit B, 215-235.

Upon our arrival on the island, we first met with Major Faw, legal counsel to General Burger. Major Faw had penned the order that initiated the court of inquiry, and he was said to be behind giving Matt the business. It seemed to me that Major Faw was doing what many lawyers do: finding legal avenues to accomplish his client's wishes. In this instance, I guessed it was the wishes of General Burger to put a distance between himself and this tragedy.

Major Faw was tall and lean with thick wavy hair controlled by a buzz cut, with greater thickness at the top of his head. He was a Texas native accustomed to the warm, humid climate of the south, and later when it came to arranging a courtroom, the absence of air conditioning was more of a burden to northerners than native southerners. In his career with the Marines, Major Faw would rise to the level of brigadier general and become director of the Judge Advocates Division from 1969 until his retirement in 1971. By 1975, he would embrace a faith based on the *Book of Urantia* in his retirement, which included concepts of channeling celestial beings.[153] That lay ahead of him. In 1956, he was squarely on earth as he shook my hand and began to compile the copies of the transcript, exhibits, and investigative materials from his desk to his arms for transfer to us.

Major Faw said he would be happy to assist in any way he could, answer any questions, and review the military code. I thanked him and said that Lieutenant Collins had been more than helpful and had answered many of our questions. He smiled as he handed us the transcript of the inquiry, which was at least two inches thick. The onion-skin paper that was commonly used in carbon copies in those days sat atop a legal-length green-cardboard back, tied at the top with a metal fastener. In the back were the exhibits: the maps and the photos of the boys' recovery from the creek, their bodies tightened as though in a defeat of a stomach punch, with fists ready to rise in a frozen boxer-like stance that is common to rigor mortis. I flipped the 154 pages back on top of the exhibits and covered the

---

153 "Duane Faw: Honoring a Man Who Served the Revelation, Saskia Praamsma, Urantia Foundation, June 1, 2008. http://www.urantia.org/news/2008. December, 2014.

photographs. I took the transcript, thanked Major Faw, and left with Jim McGarry for a night of reading testimony and digesting exhibits.

As we walked from the building toward our rooms for the night, I looked out at the lowlands of Parris Island. The water swirled in the gray-blue reflections of the sky above. Water circled the nineteen and a half square miles that make up the waterways and land that compose this training depot for the US Marines. It was acquired by the United States in 1883, first used as a prison and then for training. It is surrounded by marshes, creeks, waterways, and swamps inhabited by alligators, eastern diamond-back rattlesnakes, and venomous spiders. The air is punctuated with persistent sand fleas, gnats, and horse flies. Along the entrance of the island, a warm breeze teased the sage-moss-covered branches of the oak trees that disguised the harsh ugliness of the unforgiving lowland in its veil of camouflage beauty.

The south looked so different from home in the northeast, with so much country and so few buildings, and the few buildings out here were short, simple, and square. I commented to a passing Marine that the moss hanging from the trees looked so foreign to me but so pretty. As he walked, he turned back and warned me against too close a scrutiny of it, as it was known to carry jiggers that bite. He said it was used in the old days as stuffing for mattresses but only after the jiggers were boiled out of it and he warned that many a northerner has been seduced to its touch only to be left with its bitter bite.

CHAPTER THREE

———

APRIL 15, 1956, THE SUN had not yet risen on Saturday morning when my alarm went off at 5:00 a.m. The morning quiet was fleeting in the face of my anticipation of the long day ahead for all of us surrounded by the unyielding tides of Parris Island. I was slow to rise due to the anxious responsibility before me. A certain anxiety before a trial never goes away. This feeling before trial so sobers the spirit that it can only hear the heartbeat of what must be done to prevail: what must be asked, what must be said, what must be covered, how will they decide, and what will happen to the client who has placed his or her trust so thoroughly in my care. The early-morning quiet brings clarity to the task. The work will get done, and the evening will bring a need for relief from the burden of the day that passed. The burden is the reason we imbibe, we who belong to the club of men who need relief and find it in a cocktail.

How to deal with the alcohol? How to deal with the drinks Matt had that day? Today the prosecution would begin putting Marine brass on the stand. The first witness of the morning—Lt. Robert J. Atcheson, Medical Corps, United States Naval Reserve—would testify about the Bogen's test concerning the alcohol levels in Matt's blood. In response, I would try to elicit agreement from him by using his own reports and testimony to support my position where possible, particularly in the beginning of the cross-examination. I would try to establish with Dr. Atcheson as much helpful testimony as I could. There should be plenty.

I rose from the bed, turned on the light, showered, and dressed. My body performed each task necessary to its presentation as my mind went over the points I needed to cover.

Matt passed every clinical examination for sobriety administered to him that night. He was asked to point to an object. He did so, and he passed. He was asked to stand with his feet close together and close his eyes to test his balance. He did so, and he passed. He walked in a straight line for over twenty feet without any difficulty. His reflexes were normal; his speech was normal. He answered questions accurately and immediately. His pupils were normal. All the clinical findings noted on the examination performed by Atcheson that night were normal. Yet somehow the doctor noted that there was a clinical suggestion of alcohol, which was totally inconsistent with his clinical findings of "normal." In addition, twenty-three recruits testified at the court of inquiry, and not one of the recruits said that Matt was under the influence of alcohol. Five said he appeared normal. Two said he walked with a limp or "hitch," which he did because he had back pain and walked with a cane that night. They added that he appeared tired, very tired. McPherson said he lifted a bottle but could not say if he drank out of it. Matt told me he did not drink out of the bottle when McPherson was in the room, and I believed him. I believe him still to this day.

Yet the fact that Matt had a few drinks about seven to eight hours before the incident was a damning fact that had figured prominently in the press. The prosecution would try to maximize its damning effect. They would use it to support their theory that Matt did not have authority to conduct the march and that his judgment was somehow impaired. That was their theory, just a theory. We would maintain the opposite. We would maintain that Matt was not under the influence of alcohol. We could prove through the testimony that the drinks occurred eight hours before the incident and his clinical examination was normal without any signs of intoxication. More significantly, his authority to conduct the march was constructive, if not actual, as the night marches were part of Marine Corps training practices in the past. Matt told me that when he came through Parris Island, he was taken on a march through the swamps during his training.

Matt was not alone in his experience of marches through the swamp, and he did not concoct the idea to go out that night on a march by himself. Matt's senior drill instructor, Sgt. Edward A. Huff, was among the twenty-four witnesses who had already testified at the inquiry. Sergeant Huff testified on Wednesday, April 11. After Sergeant Huff's direct by the prosecution, the court asked him directly if he knew of or had an opinion as to whether night marches are normal. Unscheduled night marches. Sergeant Huff said he did not quite understand. He was asked about regulations that might govern night marches, and he did not know of any. The court pressed him on this and asked again:

> Question: Had you ever heard of a drill instructor taking a platoon into the swamps at night? Had you ever heard of that being done?
> Answer: Yes, sir.
> Question: How did you happen to…is that occasionally done by a drill instructor? Did you accept that as a training procedure?
> Answer: Well I don't know what other drill instructor done it or when they done it, but I know it has been done quite often since I've been here.
> Question: It has been done to your knowledge?
> Answer: I heard about it the next day.[154]

The court asked Sergeant Huff for details: Which drill sergeants? Which platoon numbers? How did he hear it? When did he hear it? Sergeant Huff only offered that he had heard it had been done and gave the court no details that would incriminate his colleagues and potentially add additional parties to this inquiry. All Sergeant Huff gave the court of inquiry was that he had heard of marches in the swamps in the First Battalion. Sergeant

---

154 Court of Inquiry Transcript, 128.

Huff was in the Third Battalion, having been transferred from the Second Battalion.[155] Sergeant Huff's testimony did not implicate any sergeants whom he knew, but he testified pretty clearly that he knew of the practice. Sergeant Huff was questioned aggressively during the inquiry:

> Question: Did you tell Sergeant McKeon that such a procedure was an acceptable thing?
> Answer: I said a lot of drill instructors do it.
> Question: Did you ever tell Sergeant McKeon that that was an accepted thing? If the platoon was goofing off?
> Answer: No, sir.
> Question: You're sure you never indicated to him that a platoon could be disciplined by being taken down to the water?
> Answer: I never said the platoon could be disciplined, but I chewed their tails off one day and I told them if they don't snap out of their hockey, I would take them in the swamps.
> Question: You told the platoon that?
> Answer: I told the platoon that. [156]

As I read Huff's testimony the night before, I hoped I could get some other Marines to testify about these marches. If a Marine, or better yet several, could testify that he participated in a night march like the one of Sunday past, then that would show the implicit authority to conduct the march. I would get to work on looking for witnesses as soon as I could, which wouldn't be until the end of testimony that day at the very earliest.

The sun was beginning to rise as I walked over for breakfast where I met Jim McGarry. We reviewed the list of anticipated witnesses for the day. Besides Dr. Atcheson, the remaining evidence would center on the tides, the rules governing training practices, and the testimony of the officers presiding that day.

---

155   Ibid., 133.
156   Ibid., 127–29.

After breakfast, I went straight to the brig to see Matt. When we first arrived on Parris Island, I could see that the jail was one of the older structures on the island. It was a large rectangular one-to-two-story brick building with two separate doors situated between four windows and bordered by two more windows at either end of the long facade. A large A-line roof sloped downward to its face. A second-story window on the side of the building suggested a storage area on a limited second floor. One of the doors had a sign over it that read: "Provost Guard." The other door was lined with bars on its interior. The brick around the entry doors was a different shade, as though added around smaller doors than the original. Beyond it, neatly kept borders stretched across the island, made of compacted sand and dirt, and with marshes and glimpses of its unfriendly water cutting into its edges. There was no place to go even if anyone could get out from behind those bars.

This jail would be Matt's home until mid-July, when they placed him on a house arrest. Until then he was confined behind several sets of bars and kept in a cool, damp cell with an iron-frame bed and thin mattress. When I saw him, he was ready to go to court, sitting on the edge of the bed, waiting to be taken in. I could not get used to the sound of the cell doors opening and closing and would never get used to seeing Matt McKeon, Anne's brother, behind bars. My travels here, my work, the help I requested of Dean Mulligan, and the help I would continue to request of senior members of the New York Bar came down to this: this jail, this man in jail, and these bars for many years.

I have never felt the same weight in any other case. Other cases I handled before that date and after concerned money damages. Criminal trials have so much more at stake. But the sound of the cell closing in your ear, the windowless cell, a future in a small space, a life broken and breaking in your hands, is a burden unlike any other.

Matt looked up as the guard approached and rose to his feet. The guard opened the cell door and let me in. Matt reached his hand out for mine and said, "Tom, thank you for coming. You did not have to."

"I know. I wanted to come."

Matt's face seemed so sad. He was tall and thin and seemed thinner still now. There was no hint of that smile I knew so well. I went over the process for the next few days, the witness list, and my hope that I might find some Marines to testify about night drills. Matt wanted to know if I had seen his wife. I had not seen anybody except Lieutenant Collins and Jim McGarry, but I assured him I would by day's end. I saw that as heavy the burden of a defense is for a trial lawyer, the burden the client bears is unknowable. I can't tell you what he said or what I said to him. Those communications are privileged, and we carry our clients' secrets to the grave, but I can tell you that after we spoke, I told him I was proud to be able to help him and proud to be his lawyer. Besides, Anne would divorce me and kick me to the curb if I didn't. He seemed to want to smile but shook his head with its hint and instead just said yes. We hardly had a half hour, and it was time to leave.

At ten minutes to eight, we walked toward the administration building and entered a side door to the building. We walked into a hallway that led to another side entry to Room 105, passing through a door jamb with a sign over the jamb that read: Defense Counsel. Matt walked in first, and I behind him. Someone took a photo of us both as we entered that I have kept in my office and later gave to my youngest daughter, Marie, the only lawyer of my children.

At 8:00 a.m., Lieutenant Collins, Jim McGarry, and I sat at the defense table with Matt in Room 105 of the administration building. Reporters filled the benches, talking and exchanging notes. In front of us sat Brig. Gen. Wallace M. Greene Jr., United States Marine Corps, presiding for his first day on Parris Island; Col. John B. Heles, United States Marine Corps; Maj. Gerald McIntyre, Marine Corps Reserve; and Lt. William Spann, Medical Corps, United States Naval Reserve. Major Holben appeared for the prosecution.

Dr. Robert Atcheson started the morning by testifying that Matt was able to point effectively to the object requested and had complete control of equilibrium in a balance test. His gait was normal, he walked in a straight line, his reflexes were normal, his speech was normal, and his pupils were normal. In spite of all the normal findings, his report noted a "suggestive odor of alcohol." He testified that his notation of clinical evidence of alcohol was not based on any clinical findings. Rather, he said, "I had asked the Sergeant during the course of the examination, which is not recorded here, if he had anything to drink in the recent past and he said yes, he had a few shots of vodka that afternoon. The statement, going along with the breath which was suggestive to me of alcohol, I had to say that there was some evidence that the patient may have been under the influence of alcohol, although my physical examination, as far as I could determine, was that he was in complete control of himself. Now, this may be confusing but I don't mean it to be because as far as I was concerned he was not intoxicated to the point of not knowing where he was or not knowing what he was doing but then again he may have been subjectively under the influence of alcohol as he admittedly had had a few drinks of vodka because his breath did smell of alcohol."[157]

There were no clinical findings of intoxication. Nonetheless, the written report offered an interpretation that Dr. Atcheson would later recant at the trial. At the inquiry, he tried to explain the inconsistency as "confusing" but alleged it was based on the defendant's statements. I asked him about the Bogen's test, a chemical sort of intoxication test, which he administered but knew little about. I brought him through all of his normal findings and ended by asking if Matt was in complete control of his faculties, to which he responded, "I have already so stated: yes, sir."

Major Holben asked a follow-up question if Dr. Atcheson's conclusions were based entirely on the Bogen's test, and Dr. Atcheson responded: "I am glad you asked me that. I think counsel over here was going along those lines, too. I, myself, seeing as I have no experience with the Bogen's test, will not make any attempt to...and have heard numerous occasions the test discredited in its entirety and I would in no respect base any of my

---

157 Ibid., 158.

impressions about the sobriety test on the Bogen's. In other words I ignored it completely."

Holben had the good sense to stop there. I was then able to cross-examine Dr. Atcheson, and I asked: "You say this Bogen's test has been discredited entirely? Is that what you said?"

"Well, as I understand, it does not stand up legally in court as a true measure of blood alcohol or whatever it is supposed to measure. In other words, it does not give an accurate picture of the percentage of alcohol."[158]

Dr. Atcheson testified that he only performed the test because he was requested or ordered to do so.

And so that is how we dealt with the alcohol issue: there was no evidence of intoxication.

After Dr. Atcheson, the prosecution called Sgt. Algin Nolan, assigned to administrative clerk—depot sergeant major, whose responsibility was to make up the tide table. His tables were based on tides in the Savannah River, to which twenty-five minutes were to be added to arrive at Parris Island tides. On April 8, 1956, the high tides occurred at 6:16 a.m. and 6:34 p.m. Sunrise occurred at 6:03 a.m. and sunset at 6:49 p.m. Living on City Island, I understood that certain tides might be higher or lower depending on the moon and hit the edge of the land differently depending on the grade of the ground below. Also, differing points along the coast and probably within Parris Island as well would have different high point times. I brought that out as best I could and asked Sergeant Nolan which point the twenty-five minutes referred to, which was Parris Point. He responded that the incident occurred between Parris Point and Archer's Creek such that an extra ten minutes would be added. The witness did not have the exact time for Ribbon Creek, nor did he have any records that indicated the depth of the water in Ribbon Creek, nor did he have any knowledge about where in Parris Island the tide charts were published.[159]

---

158 Ibid., 163–64.
159 Ibid., 165–79.

Major Holben next called Capt. Charles Weddel, depot adjutant, custodian of depot files and orders. The specific orders that Holben brought out were signed by Chief of Staff Buse as of February 1956, who read into the record various depot orders, including that the waters around Parris Island were out of bounds for swimming due to pollution.

Next Col. David Silvey offered that in training there were four authorized marches: the march back and forth to Elliot's Beach and the march from the main station to the rifle range and back again from rifle range. He also testified that ten hours of swimming instruction was offered to qualify the recruits as swimmers and to give them a limited amount of combat swimming. Colonel Silvey offered that during the march to Elliot's Beach, the recruits were to stay out of the marshes. As there was no clear prohibition against all marshes, nor any prohibition against the use of discretion by a drill instructor, I probed that area on cross-examination. After several questions wherein Captain Weddel held firm that nothing was authorized beyond what was in the plan, he finally did admit that a drill instructor has some discretion to teach discipline.[160] And then I asked:

Question: Do you have any specific orders on this post to the effect that these marsh areas or other areas are out of bounds for training purposes? If you can answer that question yes or no I would appreciate it.

Answer: I can answer it, yes, the Standard Operating Procedure for instructions at Elliot's Beach is definitely prohibited.

Question: Definitely prohibits what?

Answer: Training in swamps, where to and from and while at Elliot's Beach, for example.

Question: Do you have any instruction to that effect relative to Ribbon Creek where this incident took place?

Answer: Not to my knowledge.[161]

---

160 Ibid., 187.
161 Ibid., 188.

I asked Colonel Silvey if there were any signs posted that the area was out of bounds behind weapons battalion, and he answered he had not inspected it but admitted that men go down to the area immediately behind the butts to pull targets. I added that men also fish in the area and it is not out of bounds for fishing, and he answered again, "Not to my knowledge."

But it was on the subject of discipline that swords of witness and counsel began to cross. In the cross-examination of Colonel Silvey, the defense found itself rooted in the idea of discipline in the Marine Corps and what that meant. As I questioned Colonel Silvey, I was greatly assisted by Lieutenant Collins at this point. Lieutenant Collins used the vernacular understood by Marines. More than that, the vocabulary of the Marines engaged the heart of what was in Matt's mind, the heart of his defense, the heart of what he was trying to develop in these young men (even if misguided under all the circumstances)—the heart of what every Marine lives by that I as a private in the army, even as a prisoner of war, did not have the benefit of, and that only fellow Marines, like Lieutenant Collins, could identify in the clarion call his service would understand. It was the esprit de corps.

Question: With the permission of the court, so far the civilian counsel has asked questions of the witness and I wonder if, in this instance, possibly I might be allowed to ask the witness some questions rather than writing them out so that the civilian counsel may ask them, sir.
President: You do have the court's permission to so ask questions, provided that it is satisfactory to the party.
Question: Colonel speaking generally now, what were the purposes of this screening of the men who are perspective drill instructors? Would I be correct in assuming that this screening would be because they have a big responsibility? If they are given the job of drill instructor?[162]

---

162   Ibid., 191-192.

Colonel Silvey responded that the primary purpose of the training was to weed out those "unsuitable" or "undesirable." Here, Lieutenant Collins began to build an important foundation stone of the defense. He probed the great care of developing and choosing a drill sergeant and the great responsibility of bringing a platoon through, all questions to which Colonel Silvey and any Marine would respond affirmatively to. He brought the witness to yes, to the things that can be agreed upon, and from there he took him to the place in the cross-examination that was more nuanced with less disagreement.

Question: Colonel I'd like to ask you a couple of questions. This word discipline has been fanned around a little bit. Now a drill instructor, on accession, does some things with a platoon that seem to be, well, we'll say seem to be of a disciplinary nature—in a punishment form. However, they also can be construed as instilling discipline, possibly. Has the Colonel ever seen a recruit running around the drill field with a rifle over his head?

Answer: Yes I have.

Question: Now that could be given two interpretations; as to whether that would be a disciplinary measure or possibly instilling discipline.

Answer: Discipline is not punishment. Now again, I say that there is only one person in the battalion that can give any form of disciplinary action and that's the battalion commander.

Question: Now referring to discipline as a punishment that is not discipline as we understand it here?

Answer: I haven't been using the word discipline as punishment at all.

Question: While there is punishment that is given by the battalion commander, how about the actual teaching of the platoon?

Answer: Well, we have at the moment two company officers for five platoons and things like that.

Question: Does the teaching of discipline rest upon whom?

Answer: In the 12 hours of Military Customs, Courtesy. And Discipline. Included in that is the subject of discipline and what it is.

Question: In actuality, all the recruits that are taught discipline down here, do they get that discipline solely from this 12 hours?

Answer: I think a man achieves orderly conduct while he is out drilling. He is taught how to stand at attention properly. He is taught how to drill and he practices. He is corrected by his drill instructor if he makes a mistake and he practices again...something that is true of close order drill; you practice a movement and you practice it and you practice it under the command of the drill instructor who gives the command of execution. And a man must learn to obey orders and follow them automatically. Then you are achieving orderly conduct within a platoon and within the squads.

Question: Sir, would you say that possibly the end of the recruit training is the discipline...I mean the big end...that you might encompass the spirit of the Corps...the military courtesy...things of that nature?

Answer: Yes it would encompass Spirit of the Corps. As a matter of fact I would say that a platoon that graduates from Parris Island has a very high degree of platoon pride and pride for the Marine Corps.[163]

Lieutenant Collins illustrated that there was a necessary discretion to the work of a drill sergeant and that there was an important distinction between instilling discipline versus administering it. Colonel Silvey was not venturing into the territory that Lieutenant Collins was taking him. Eventually it would take a much higher-ranking officer to actually offer precise testimony first sought by Lieutenant Collins that day as to whether

---

163   Ibid., 191–93.

or not the night march was a good practice for instilling discipline, but that testimony would not come until much later during the trial.

The work of the day was not nearly finished. After we broke for lunch, we took more testimony from Captain Chiappetti, who testified about the training of drill sergeants. As to Matt in particular, Captain Chiappetti said he was an above-average graduate from drill-instructor school. None of the officers who testified so far would budge on the issue of the swamp being off limits by virtue of the Elliot's Beach prohibition, which was not directed to Ribbon Creek—none except for Colonel McKean.

Prior to taking the stand that Saturday, Colonel McKean spent the week searching for bodies and searching for regulations. In 1958, Dial Press published Colonel McKean's recollections of that night and the trial in a book that is now out of publication entitled: *Ribbon Creek*. I read it when it first came out, and it provided a background on this critical point of whether Ribbon Creek was off limits. I wish I could have known on that Saturday morning that within less than a month of testifying and within three months of his retirement, Colonel McKean would lose his command. Given the timing, I suspected that his testimony that Saturday may have had something to do with his removal. The prosecution would not call him again as a witness at the trial.

For Colonel McKean, this tragedy started on Sunday evening, April 8, 1956. Colonel McKean, the commander of weapons battalion, was watching *The Ed Sullivan Show* with his wife. At age forty-seven, he was four months shy of retiring after twenty-seven years of service. He was square jawed, square shouldered, and square chinned, with a reserve of fiercely independent military resolve running through his blue blood that he proudly traced to family members who included a signer of the Declaration of Independence and Franklin Buchanan, who commanded the Confederate States Navy.[164] Pride may have invited his pending retirement. Colonel McKean had been passed over by a selection board at Marine headquarters for promotion to brigadier general and was not chosen by General Burger

---

164   McKean, *Ribbon Creek*, 241.

for depot chief of staff in January 1956 when Burger assumed command of Parris Island.[165]

Sunday night was interrupted by a call from Captain Patrick, officer of the day at Parris Island, notifying Colonel McKean of trouble. Colonel McKean responded to the call with the order to "Lock up the DI."[166] The immediacy of the directive without any investigative support came within moments of the platoon's arrival in their barracks. Sergeant McKeon was still wet and muddy when the MP arrived to execute Colonel McKean's order. The MP allowed Matt to change his shirt and shoes to dry ones before heading out to the brig.

Colonel McKean returned to his den. The words "swamp," "lost," "missing," and "lock up the DI" did not alert him. [167]He was not overly concerned. A search party, a matter-of-fact proceeding to follow, a court-martial, and a plea taken soon after would square it all away. Colonel McKean's thoughts were orderly, resolute, and simple. He thought the missing recruits were lost.[168] He decided to go to Parris Island to check on the status. As he backed out of his driveway, his thoughts wandered to his pending retirement and the utility bills that would soon become his own.[169]

Colonel McKean drove out to C Butts. He parked and observed patrol cars, a resuscitator with an operator, an ambulance, and a fire engine. He asked about the need for a resuscitator and was told Depot Chief of Staff Buse wanted it out in case they needed it.[170] Although Colonel McKean was second in authority to General Burger, the position of depot chief of staff was held by the number-three officer in authority at Parris Island, Col. Henry Buse Jr.[171]

---

165 Fleming, *U.S. Marine Corps in Crisis*, 32.

166 See note 143 above.

167 Court of Inquiry Transcript, 223.

168 Ibid.

169 McKean, *Ribbon Creek*, 12.

170 Ibid., 14.

171 Fleming, *U.S. Marine Corps in Crisis*, 32–38.

As Colonel McKean and Depot Chief of Staff Buse spoke, a recruit from North Carolina, Clarence Cox, approached them walking through the four-foot-tall reeds in the marsh of Ribbon Creek. Cox was soaking wet and had mud on his jacket. Other than the appearance of cold, he appeared to Colonel McKean to be in good shape for someone who just walked out of the creek. Cox had swam to the other side and crossed over again after he heard the rescuers calling. As he approached, Colonel McKean asked him how he felt. He said, all right. He asked if there was anyone else around him and Cox said no, he had gotten lost from the platoon and was by himself. [172]

Colonel McKean surveyed the rescue searchers with lights scanning the black ebbing waters of the creek. A resuscitator waited, unused. Cold night air started to penetrate Colonel McKean's light jacket. Captain Patrick returned to Colonel McKean and said Father Bielski was mad that he was not notified.

> "McKean responded, 'We don't need a chaplain. It isn't that kind of emergency...' "[173]

It all seemed under control to Colonel McKean and he decided to go home at approximately 11:30. He testified at the Court of Inquiry that he "sensed no real emergency" and was just about to go to bed when the chief of staff called and said the general was worried and was coming out. [174]

Maj. Gen. Joseph C. Burger, commanding officer of Marine Corps Recruits Depot, Parris Island, in January 1956 had spent that Sunday in Augusta Georgia, watching a golf tournament, and upon returning home he had gone to bed early. [175] General Burger was awakened by a call from Colonel Buse who told him that six recruits were missing, no one knew yet if they had drowned, and it would "probably be morning before they knew for sure." [176] General Burger decided to dress and head out to Parris Island.

---

172   Court of Inquiry Transcript, 223.
173   McKean, *Ribbon Creek,* 15.
174   Court of Inquiry Transcript, 223.
175   Fleming, *U.S. Marine Corps in Crisis,* 37.
176   Ibid., 32, 38.

At approximately midnight, Colonel McKean was at home. If he had heard the word "drowned" that night, it is missing from his recorded recollections of the evening and missing from his sworn testimony offered at the inquiry. As the long night turned to midnight, his plan of sleep was topped off with a nightcap with his wife. As the couple were about to go up the stairs to their bedroom, the phone rang again. It was Depot Chief Buse. He said that General Burger was worried and was going out to Parris Island. McKean said he would meet them there.[177] McKean recorded in his memoir, *Ribbon Creek*, that as he hung up the phone, he thought: *What the hell's the old man worried about? Of course he's new on the job—hasn't been here three months yet. After he's been around longer, he'll find out this is mere routine.*[178]

Colonel McKean returned to Parris Island where he met General Burger and Depot Chief Buse. They parked behind C Butts and walked out into the night toward the creek where activity remained focused on locating the missing recruits. They met Major McLeod, who provided an update based upon statements from Sergeant McKeon.[179]

Major McLeod learned from Sergeant McKeon the exact location of the occurrence so that the search efforts could be targeted more precisely.[180] He advised Depot Chief Buse, General Burger, and Colonel McKean that Sergeant McKeon said that he had gone straight out from the target shed in C Butts and entered the creek up to his chest. He made a column left and traveled up stream parallel to the river bank.[181] Major McLeod added that "some of his boys started yelling-maybe in the dark they got a little panicky-and he lost control."[182] This was the first time the words "panicky" and "a panic" were used to describe what happened that Sunday night, but it would not be the last. The word "panic" would be heard throughout the

---

177   Court of Inquiry Transcript, 223.
178   McKean, *Ribbon Creek*, 20.
179   Ibid.
180   Court of Inquiry Transcript, 118–19.
181   Ibid.
182   McKean, *Ribbon Creek*, 20.

trial. Panic is a sudden sensation of fear that is so strong that it prevents reason. The word panic is derived from the Greek word referring to the god Pan, who enjoyed frightening herds of animals into frenzied bursts of uncontrollable fear. Pan also directed his efforts at soldiers who in frantic fear would be caused to flee a battlefield, as in the ancient Battle of Marathon. On April 8, 1956, the platoon panicked.

I imagine General Burger listened silently, taking in the darkness pierced by the occasional roaming of solitary lights of a search-and-rescue team. One man was dead, maybe more. He calculated a response, which the hour of the night delayed. There would be a criminal inquiry. Tomorrow morning he would have to brief the commandant of the Marine Corps, General Pate. He counted the hours left until daybreak: approximately five. This meant five hours until a report would have to be sent to headquarters. Colonel McKean and General Burger agreed to get a written statement from the DI and to get the DI out here on the field to narrow the search area. Colonel McKean watched the headlights of the general's car pull away from the quiet contemplation still lingering after his departure. [183]

Major McLeod again sent for Sergeant McKeon for the second time that night, with a "prison chaser" following.[184] Sergeant McKeon appeared tall and lean, wearing freshly starched utilities, hair cropped tight to the head, in a fine "example for any recruit."[185] The sergeant's expression was serious, and his demeanor calm. Sergeant McKeon was a trained combat veteran and a trained educator in weaponry who knew how to communicate in adverse circumstances.

Sergeant McKeon reiterated slowly that they entered the creek behind C Butts, they turned left in the creek, right, and left again, and then some of the boys became panicky. Some jumped on his back. One, a section leader, jumped on him. They struggled. He did not see him again.

---

183 McKean, *Ribbon Creek*, 21.

184 Ibid., 24.

185 Ibid.

Colonel McKean's suspicion of men lost in the flatlands surrounding the creek was premature. The recruits were not simply missing or lost. He began to realize he was not looking for wanderers but for corpses, six of them.[186] Colonel McKean ordered Captain Patrick to have all the boats manned and out at daylight. There would not be any weapons training until all the recruits were found. In morning it would be high tide, and they could see over all the flats and would surely find them then.[187]

Colonel McKean remained behind C Butts as Major McLeod took Sergeant McKeon to the creek to point out the area where his platoon last saw the missing men. I imagine that Colonel McKean assessed the night and days before him through the lens of an incomplete conclusion that incorrectly altered his perceptions of what lay ahead. He thought Sergeant McKeon should be immediately peremptorily separated from the Marine Corps through court-martial, wherein an undesirable discharge could be accepted in lieu of trial or an undesirable discharge issued after a court of inquiry was convened. It was a simple plan, one that Colonel McKean later recommended to the chief of staff. Colonel McKean thought Chief of Staff Buse gave it the "brush off."[188]

Colonel McKean's plan to "lock up the DI" and end it quickly was a plan that did not ask a lot of questions and did not anticipate a defense. It was not a plan that needed a broken regulation. It was not a plan that imagined a relief of command for Colonel McKean. I further imagine that as Colonel McKean sized up Sergeant McKeon's haircut, starched utilities, and calm demeanor, he could not see that he and this drill sergeant from New England were not so different and that one was diminished with the other. He did not see me in Matt's life, a brother-in-law who was a lawyer. He could not see or have anticipated in the dark of that night a group of judges in New York who would be sympathetic to a criminal trial so far away, or sympathetic to the criminally accused. Colonel McKean

---

186 Ibid.

187 Ibid.

188 McKean, *Ribbon Creek*, 531–33.

was tired. He dismissed Major McLeod and Sergeant McKeon and went home until the morning twilight woke him to the obligation of finding six Marines at the bottom of a creek bed.

By morning the search had not brought any results. General Burger notified General Pate of this by 7:45 a.m. The message relayed across the halls of the southwest end of the navy annex in Washington, DC, was that there was a tragedy on Parris Island. This message reached Gen. Randolph Pate at his alma mater, the Virginia Military Institute in Lexington, Virginia, where he was to give a speech. He left immediately to travel to Parris Island. At headquarters in Washington, information management was supervised in part by Col. James Hittle, who was legislative assistant to key members of Congress, including supporters of the Marine Corps from the House of Representatives and Senate. Hittle informed members of Congress before they heard it from the press.[189] A terse press release drafted at headquarters was issued at 1:00 p.m. on Monday, April 9, 1956, and indicated that six Marines were missing from Parris Island after a night exercise.[190] This caused Parris Island to be inundated with calls and newsmen.

Colonel McKean returned to Parris Island in the morning to wait for the waters of Ribbon Creek to give up its dead. Helicopters searched overhead, and boats dredged the bottom of the creek bed. The first body was recovered at 1:00 p.m.—at about the same time as the press release. It appeared to be Recruit Wood, who was last seen by Sergeant McKeon. Colonel McKean's worst fears were realized. He thought that the DI has had it and damned if the "whole Marine Corps has had it too!"[191]

On the morning of April 9, 1956, General Burger ordered the court of inquiry to "inquire into the circumstances surrounding the marching of Platoon 71, Third Recruit Training Battalion, into the swamps adjacent to weapons Training Battalion on April 8, 1956 and the disappearance of Private Thomas Hardeman, 1587021, USMC; Private First Class Donald

---

189 Fleming, *U.S. Marine Corps in Crisis*, 40–43.

190 Ibid., 42.

191 McKean, *Ribbon Creek*, 108.

Francis O'Shea, 1550900, USMC; Private Charles Francis O'Reilly, 15566628, USMC; Private Jerry Lamonte Thomas, 1585496, USMC; Private Leroy Thompson, 1590031, USMC; and Private Norman Alfred Wood, 1590034, USMC."[192]

By 4:40 p.m. of April 9, five bodies had been recovered from Ribbon Creek. Colonel McKean witnessed the retrieval of each of the five bodies. He watched Father Tony Bielski pray over each body, although he recorded in his memoir, *Ribbon Creek*, that it did not escape his attention that only one of the deceased wore a Catholic medal.[193] Nonetheless, he thought there might be some solace for the families in a prayer, even if in a Catholic one.

Corpsmen who worked the recovery turned their faces away in sadness at the recovered bodies that bore the signs of drowning in the goose-like bumps of their skin and the desperation of the clenched fists stiffened in place by rigor mortis. One of the Marines involved in the recovery turned away to weep when he got off the boat that had been involved in recovering four of the bodies.[194] At 4:30 p.m. that day, a fifth body was recovered as General Pate and General Burger met on the island. The sixth body was still missing.

The generals of Parris Island looked for a depot order that made Ribbon Creek out of bounds for everyone.[195] They could not find one. They must have hoped that Colonel McKean could point them to such an order that they could reference in the upcoming press conference because General Pate and General Burger drove to where Colonel McKean was overseeing recovery operations to ask him. A news conference was already overdue, and the reporters were waiting for the details to fill in the cursory 1:00

192 Record of Proceedings of a Court of Inquiry convened at Marine Corps Recruit Depot Parris Island, South Carolina by Order of Commanding General, Marine Corps Recruit Depot, Parris Island, South Carolina, Ordered on April 9, 1956, title page.

193 McKean, *Ribbon Creek*, 110.

194 Ibid., 108–14.

195 Fleming, *U.S. Marine Corps in Crisis*, 43.

p.m. report. The reporters needed to get the story written and printed for the morning papers.

The general's car passed Colonel McKean as he stood at attention watching their official car drive by him, "four stars flying."[196] After that "wave off," Colonel McKean walked less hurriedly to where the general's car had stopped some 250 yards ahead of him, in spite of knowing that protocols would require a faster pace.[197] This "wave off" by General Pate was the first of several slights that Colonel McKean would suffer and later ruefully record in his memoir, *Ribbon Creek*.

As Colonel McKean approached General Pate standing outside his car with General Burger, they shook hands, and he was asked by General Pate whether any depot orders prohibited a night exercise like this one. McKean could not recall any, but Pate urged further:

"There has to be something to cover this."

McKean said: "There may be—I hope so—but I haven't had much time since last night to read orders. I am going to study them when I get this job finished. Right now I'm talking off the cuff but I can't stand here and lie to you. To the best of my recollection we have no order that covers a deal like this."[198]

It was not the answer General Pate was hoping for. Shortly thereafter General Pate held a press conference where he intended to make a statement that he planned with General Burger. The planned statement refrained from making charges until after the court of inquiry completed its investigation. The court of inquiry was to convene on Tuesday, April 10, 1956.[199] The prepared statement went well until General Pate took questions from the press. With television cameras in his eyes, General Pate

---

196 McKean, *Ribbon Creek*, 113.
197 Ibid.
198 Ibid.
199 Fleming, *U.S. Marine Corps in Crisis*, 44.

accused the drill sergeant of malpractice; he "practically accused him of manslaughter" and of being drunk, even though there was no evidence to support those conclusions at that time.[200]

The press asked, "General, did the drill sergeant break any regulations?"

General Pate answered, "It would appear so."

General Burger watched the press conference and concluded that General Pate "had for all practical purposes accused McKeon of manslaughter before the Court of Inquiry even convened."[201] Colonel McKean later heard the reports and still could not find a specific regulation prohibiting the swamp area. Nor could he find that sought-after regulation by Saturday morning, April 14, 1956, when he was called to testify.

Colonel McKean took the stand on Saturday, less than a week after he had been sitting in his home office on a Sunday evening. Within six days of being informed by Captain Patrick that there was trouble at weapons battalion, he was sitting on a witness stand, under oath, about to give testimony. He was proud. He opened with a statement before anyone could ask a question. He said:

> I am the commanding officer of Weapons Training Battalion. I had jurisdiction over the area and the people involved in this incident. A commanding officer is responsible for everything that his unit does or fails to do. I am fully aware of my rights under the Constitution and the revised statutes of the United States. I wish to waive any right to be named as a party to this inquiry. I wish to waive any rights subsidiary thereto, such as being present, having counsel, calling and examining witnesses or any restriction that there might be on my own testimony. It is not my intention during this inquiry to claim the personal privilege of refusing to answer any question which I feel may be incriminating. I am ready to go

---

200   Ibid., citing Lt. Gen. Joseph C. Burger Oral History Transcript, 1969 (Oral History Collection, Marine Corps Historical Center, Washington, D.C., 291, 201–2.

201   See note 199 above.

ahead. May I add that my sole interest is to see the truth developed by this inquiry as expeditiously as possible.[202]

Colonel McKean testified that in the thirty-three months since he was stationed at Parris Island, he had participated in the training of seventy-six thousand recruits. He was asked if there was any area authorized for swimming in the weapons battalion area, and he responded that swimming was prohibited in the waters around Parris Island.[203] Colonel McKean then described his notice of the accident a little before ten on Sunday night and the recovery efforts that enlisted the aid of the local sheriff for grapnels, local fire department, local shrimpers familiar with the water and with ready boats, a helicopter search by the Georgia National Guard, and Marines who dove, built grapnels of their own, dragged the waters below, prayed, and recovered the bodies of six recruits.

On cross-examination during the court of inquiry, I asked Colonel McKean if in all the orders he testified to, "in any of those orders is there any specific prohibition from using the marsh and swamp areas for a training exercise?"[204] He answered that he was not aware of all the orders in evidence, but he was "willing to answer this question and I believe it is what you want to get out of me. To the best of my knowledge the only order that relates to swamps has to do with marching down around in the area of Elliot's Beach. That is available from the records and I am testifying from memory."[205]

Colonel McKean testified that there had been a rash of marching around the area of Elliot's Beach and the order prohibiting training near Elliot's Beach was directed to stop that activity. I asked him:

---

202 Court of Inquiry Transcript, 215.
203 Ibid., 221.
204 Ibid., 226.
205 Ibid.

Question: So then as far as any Depot Orders provided to you, Colonel, relating to the use of these marsh areas for training purposes or otherwise, the only prohibited area was this Elliot's Beach area and that was specifically prohibited?

Answer: To the best of my recollection.

Question: And on the date when this incident took place, April 8th of this year, that was the fact. In other words, there hadn't been any new standard operating procedure which prohibited any other marsh area?

Answer: To the best of my recollection that is true.[206]

I asked him if he had any maps of the area, and he described several, none of which included the creek bed itself. I asked him if he had a map of the conditions of the creek that might include a hole, and he said, "no, any information I might have had would have come from local fishermen. I personally have no information that would indicate holes or otherwise."[207]

I asked about information on tidal currents, and Colonel McKean did what every lawyer warns his or her clients to avoid. He volunteered much more than he was asked.

I have been provided with no formal information of tidal currents. Currently I wouldn't know how I'd use it if I was given it. It's rather irrelevant so far as my own job is concerned. I do have what's transmitted to me formally. I have a large number of people in my outfit who are fishermen and good watermen and right in here we have a little boat basin. We have six or eight small boats. We have ten outboard motors as I remember and we use this as a base for fishing, all that in the Broad River. This is where we got the boats for that night when we needed them on recovery. This channel up in here was dredged very recently. Just when it was dredged was a

---

206   Ibid., 227.
207   Ibid., 228.

matter of record, but it's only been a month since they've had their dredge out there.[208]

It was the word "fishing" in his response that stood out to me. If they fished in Ribbon Creek, then it certainly was not out of bounds. I asked, "Was there ever any fishing in Ribbon Creek?"

> Answer: Yes sir all the time. Not when we are firing, but Sundays, Saturday afternoon and some night fishing is done. They get down here either here or more generally down this road and they fish anywhere from Dog Butts around. They also fish from boats in Ribbon Creek.
> Question: Now these people that fish in there, are they personnel from the base here? Members of the Marine Corps, enlisted men, non-commissioned officers and officers?
> Answer: They are base personnel and local fishermen and the best fisherman around here is Mrs. Berkley who is the wife of a retired major general and is about eighty years old.[209]

Ribbon Creek began to sound a little less threatening. I continued:
> Question: Then as far as at least for the purposes of recreation, for the purpose of fishing, this area was definitely not out of bounds for use by Marine personnel?
> Answer: That is correct.
> Question: Now did anyone ever go swimming in that area, that Ribbon Creek area at about the place this incident happened?
> Answer: Not to my knowledge, frankly I know of none at all. It would be most undesirable and there is a general prohibition against swimming in these waters around Parris Island.[210]

---

208 Ibid.
209 Ibid.
210 Ibid.

Colonel McKean answered that the creek was "unpleasant"—which does not mean dangerous or menacing, just "unpleasant." I then asked:

> Question: In the thirty-three months that you were in charge of this area, did you have in any of those orders that came down from the depot for the battalion orders any specific prohibition with relation to using the swamp area around Ribbon Creek for marching purposes?"
> Answer: I know of no specific prohibition in writing.[211]

Colonel McKean asked to explain his response and testified to his philosophy regarding orders, which was to make them less specific and more streamlined. He said there were numerous orders if someone could do the research, but to the best of his recollection, he knew of nothing that would prohibit marching in the swamp of Ribbon Creek. But on the other hand, he also offered that if he knew of it, he would charge the man with maltreatment under Article 134 of the Uniform Code, which he said "is a catch-all."[212]

Colonel McKean made some points I thought were helpful to the defense, albeit unintentionally. He confirmed that the teaching of discipline was a matter of discretion within the discretion of the DI, that marching was helpful to teach discipline, and that they sometimes night marched to the movies or church, but he would not expect a night march exercise. He elaborated that he used to have a liaison officer who inspected the area at night. I sensed some discontent within him that he no longer had this position in his budget, and so I asked about it. He said that he felt much better in those days when he had a liaison officer on duty down in the area and that the reason he "added a commander of the guard to my organization sometime last fall was because I overworked my officer of the day and lacking the services from the Liaison Duty Officer."[213]

---

211 Ibid.
212 Court of Inquiry Transcript, 229.
213 Ibid., 230.

When I asked if the reason he did not think he had a tragedy at first was because he thought the area was safe, he responded that he would have been willing to try to ford Ribbon Creek in the past and had seen recruits who were attempting to leave and emerge from the creek all muddy and mosquito bitten, but of those occasions: "all that I ever heard of came back. We also since I have been here have had several rescue operations people out in boats and so forth. On at least two occasions I can think of now. They involved my own people, and they always came back."[214]

When I asked if the teaching of discipline was important, he answered: "Yes, sir. Of course the drill instructors have that idea of teaching discipline to the recruits. There is no doubt about that."[215]

McKean agreed that everything the Marines do is intended to teach discipline and that a drill sergeant has a certain amount of discretion with which to teach that discipline. I asked if the platoon had walked the line as indicated on one of the maps showing their path, whether they may have seen a sentry and not been stopped. He answered, "Yes, these posts are close in here and I guess that blue line is it," and "a platoon could go down there without being challenged. Without any question of being challenged and without any question of sentries doing their duties."[216] I asked him prior to this occurrence if he had heard of any bad currents, and he said: "No, but I think the words to describe them as I have observed them are somewhat exaggerated. I don't think the current is particularly bad."[217]

The judges asked Colonel McKean some questions, in particular why he ordered the DI to be locked up. He said it was because he thought it was maltreatment and he wanted to separate the DI from the recruits so that he could not influence them.

Colonel McKean left the stand. He had testified truthfully. Before taking the stand, he had told General Pate that he did not know of any specific

---

214 Ibid.
215 Ibid.
216 Ibid., 232.
217 Ibid., 233.

order that covered "a deal like this." His answers were not any different under oath.

In his memoir, *Ribbon Creek*, Colonel McKean wrote that he had asked fifteen to twenty weapons battalion Marines standing near the pier as they prepared for another drag to recover the bodies whether those who had trained on Parris Island (all but two) had been marched at night into the swamps of Parris Island. "The show of hands was a clear majority." He then asked these fifteen to twenty Marines that if asked to testify, how many could testify that fellow recruits had been marched through swamps during boot training. He wrote, "The show of hands was unanimous. Staff Sergeant Fotner claimed he had that experience virtually every night."[218]

Colonel McKean also wrote that he told General Burger about his informal poll on Tuesday, April 10, as they waited for the recovery efforts to be completed.[219] On the same day General Burger heard of this common practice of night marches as evidenced by the show of hands observed by Colonel McKean, he issued a convening order with a net wide enough to catch more than Sergeant McKeon and threatening enough to entangle anyone who might offer any sworn testimony that night exercises in the creek were a common and accepted practice. The order included the authority to investigate and include others in the proceedings. The order had the chilling effect to dissuade further acknowledgment of night marches by any Marine, including those who had raised their hands in response to Colonel McKean when he asked about them.

We tried to find Marines to admit to the practice, but we could not get a single Marine to agree to testify to that he had seen or had participated in night march exercises. I thought the reason was that the convening order was so broad as to invite implication of anyone who might testify about the night marches. This piece of the defense would not quite come together until later, but the themes of the defense took shape on that first Saturday after we arrived from the night train out of New York. Colonel McKean

---

218 McKean, *Ribbon Creek*, 229–30.
219 Ibid., 230.

in his memoir put it this way: just when the inquiry "could have been but-toned up, Thomas P. Costello and James P. McGarry were introduced as additional counsel for the Defendant. Thereafter, the Inquiry was directed toward Parris Island: regulations, procedures, training, customs, practices, and command relations—responsibility."[220]

I did not know that as we were traveling to Parris Island and preparing the defense, a back story in Washington was also examining "procedures, customs, practices, and command relations—responsibility." *U.S. Marine Corps in Crisis*, written by Keith Fleming in 1988, indicates that in April of 1956, US Senator Vinson, a staunch supporter of the Marines, expect-ed that the Marines take some responsibility. At the same time, General Twining, commander of Marine training on the West Coast, was called to Washington, DC, by General Pate on Monday, April 9, 1956. General Twining reviewed pages of complaints of training brutality from families and recruits. Ultimately, the Marines were concerned that a trial might bring these complaints to the public scrutiny.

As we presented evidence at the inquiry and attempted to track down witnesses concerning night marches, we did not know that General Pate would report to the secretary of the navy after the findings of the inquiry: "in a very real sense the Marine Corps is on trial for the tragedy of Ribbon Creek just as surely as is Sergeant McKeon." Nor could I know that Colonel McKean would be relieved of his command on May 2, 1956, within a week of when the findings of the inquiry were signed by General Pate.

I only knew that when I looked at Matt at the end of the day, we had done our best and offered him some hope against a maximum prison term of ten years that a manslaughter conviction might bring. We had done the work we set out to. We had met our obligations as defense counsel and had asked the right questions. I knew that when I saw his wife, Betty; his mother, Alice; his father, Daddy Jim (as Anne liked to call her father); his sister, Ellen; and his brothers, Jimmy, Ned, and Franny as I did that night, that I could look them squarely in the eye with confidence that I had

---

220 Ibid., 211.

given them my best efforts and work, and that those efforts would make a difference—a difference that might not be felt right away but would be felt in the months to come in shaping the defense. For the first time, at the end of testimony of the court of inquiry, there was a fighting chance in a process that was otherwise "buttoned up."

CHAPTER FOUR

WE WORKED THE WHOLE DAY on Sunday, April 15, 1956. After I met with Matt and reviewed the area of Ribbon Creek with him, we had lunch and then were back in the makeshift courtroom. At 1:05 p.m., the court of inquiry reconvened and continued taking testimony. We had time to eat, to sleep, and to worship, after which we returned to the inquiry where we remained working until 5:32 p.m. Three officers testified. By Monday afternoon, the medical examiner and a chain-of-custody witness on the bottle of vodka would offer evidence, and the Marines case would be finished.

Sunday's first witness was the officer of the day, Captain Patrick. His duties were to inspect and maintain control of recruits in the weapons battalion training area that was a mile and a half long by three quarters of a mile wide. Captain Patrick conducted three to four inspections a day of the area. He confirmed that there was no express regulation or prohibition of base personnel from the area behind Charlie Butts, specifically Ribbon Creek.[221] His testimony was fairly brief, because he did not see Platoon Seventy-One that night prior to responding to the scene after the call he received at approximately nine fifteen that evening. When he arrived at Ribbon Creek, he saw the platoon coming from the creek in various different formations, scattered and bedraggled. He also saw Sergeant McKeon, whom he only spoke to briefly. Captain Patrick asked if any of the platoon members were missing, and Sergeant McKeon answered yes,

----

221 Court of Inquiry Transcript, 245–53.

he thought some were. He told Sergeant McKeon to return to barracks and called Colonel McKean within five minutes of that conversation. Colonel McKean ordered that Sergeant McKeon be arrested.[222]

Colonel Thompson testified after Captain Patrick. Colonel Thompson's testimony was notable for his admission that the only reference to a swamp-marsh prohibition was applicable to Elliot's Beach, not Ribbon Creek. Colonel Thompson also did not have jurisdiction over the weapons battalion area.

We continued to probe an important theme to the defense concerning the drill instructors' discretion to instill and teach discipline. The distinction between teaching discipline and administering it was the all the difference between the Marines' theory of the case and ours. Colonel Thompson had been prepared by Major Holben for questions concerning the limitations on the training a drill instructor could employ. Our questions included that area of a drill sergeant's discretion.

Question: Your testimony then is that the drill instructor cannot go outside these specific instructions as laid down. Is that right?
Answer: Not legally that is correct.
Question: Now it is mentioned in some orders to the effect that the drill instructor has the right to give extra instructions. Do you know anything about it?
Answer: That is included in Depot General Order 348 and also extra instructions—they specify those.
Question: Your examples are already given are they not Colonel?
Answer: That is correct.
Question: Are these the only examples of those extra instructions Colonel?
Answer: I should say that they are not the only examples—however, I should like to add that I think they point out the trend of the extra instructions which they desire to be given.

---

222 Ibid.

Question: ...There are others?

Answer: There are others.

Question: Now does the drill instructor...he determines what these others are at his own discretion, is that correct sir?

Answer: As to the needs of his platoon, I would say that is correct.[223]

A tension developed between the extent of a drill instructor's discretion and the Marine Corps' theory that Sergeant McKeon broke regulations as first articulated by General Pate's premature pronouncement less than a week ago. The Corps attorney Major Holben was searching for a broken regulation from the witnesses he presented, but none could find any regulation that expressly barred the area of Ribbon Creek. An uncertain reliance upon depot orders was attempted to illustrate that all training drills were scheduled and the drill sergeant could not institute an exercise of his own. Relying on the depot orders did not hold up in cross, since Colonel Thompson admitted that there were other extra instructions that may be permissible and which were not included on the list. But the suggestion that a drill sergeant had no leeway and could not discipline a platoon or institute a training schedule would begin to cause discontent among the Corps and veteran Marines.

On our cross-examination, we probed the adequacy of staffing and supervision on Parris Island. Our questions also brought out the broad and over vague definition of maltreatment of troops that was contained in the training manual. The "Drill Instructor School Manual," Marine Corps Recruit Depot, Parris Island, South Carolina, page 3, stated:

What is maltreatment? Unnecessary rough physical or mental treatment, ask yourself if the action I am contemplating is designed to hurt the recruit for past misdeeds or to ensure his future compliance to my authority, if the answer is yes, don't do it. Now some

---

223 Ibid.

few will want a further definition of hurt, the only answer is: Do it to yourself; if it hurts, it's hurt.

When asked about that definition, Colonel Thompson just couldn't agree with the manual's definition of hurt. Nonetheless, that was the language contained in the manual. It was a definition he distanced himself from by saying that he just could not agree. The tactic of distancing the Marines from their own training and drill sergeants charged with the duty of training would backfire on them in the public eye. It would also form the basis of the trial strategy later developed by Emile Zola Berman of relying on the training practices as sound.

Capt. Richard P. Grey was the third and final witness on Sunday. He was captain of A Company, Third Recruit Training Battalion, Parris Island, South Carolina. On cross-examination, the captain also admitted that the drill sergeants had some discretion to teach discipline. I asked:

Question: Now I believe you mentioned something about a drill instructor having a right to give the men some extra activities and extra activities may cover a multitude of items. For example extra activities might cover items that are not specifically covered in a Standard Operating Procedure?
Answer: The drill instructor is encouraged to see that his platoon is gainfully occupied at all times.
Question: And the particular portion that of the standard operating procedure that I refer to is that he could during free time utilize his platoon in such things as physical conditioning?
Answer: Physical conditioning that is one that is included.
Question: And it is again in his discretion to decide what these extra activities shall be?
Answer: It is.[224]

---

224 Ibid., 292.

The questioning continued, and Major Holben had some rebuttal questions for Captain Grey. Major Holben asked:

> Question: Now referring to extra instructions you have had from experience at Parris Island in training recruits as to what extra instruction is carried out, in your opinion, based on your experience is a night march into a tidal stream within the scope of extra instruction described in Depot General Order 348?
>
> Answer: I would not consider it such.
>
> Question: What would you consider it?
>
> Answer: I have no ready definition for what I would consider it other than something that is unusual and something that I have not heard of before and would never expect to be done. If Sergeant McKeon thought he was justified in doing that, then in my opinion I would have considered it as coming under the heading of extra activities.[225]

Captain Grey also gave a favorable estimation of Matt's abilities. Captain Grey was asked whether he had the opportunity to evaluate Staff Sergeant McKeon, and he answered that he had made comments to others, such as, "I thought he was one of the smartest drill instructors we had in the battalion since I had been there."[226] His response helped the Marines in that it confirmed the justifiable confidence that the Marine Corps had in Matt. It was testimony that was favorable to both of us. It at once showed that the Marine Corps had no way of predicting the tragedy because the drill sergeant involved was exemplary up to this point. The court adjourned at 5:32 p.m. on Sunday evening.

On Monday morning, before closing arguments, Major Holben would bring three more Marines in a supervisory capacity to Matt who offered testimony of how conscientious Matt was and how generous he was with

---

225 Ibid., 296–7.
226 Ibid., 284.

the platoon by offering them breaks and water during exercises. It was helpful, but it also happened to be true. Matt was exemplary. He was smart. He was kind. At the trial, every recruit of Platoon Seventy-One would testify to that because Emile Zola Berman would close his cross-examination of each witness with a series of questions eliciting their opinion of Matt. Major Holben may have used this to exculpate the Marines in the inquiry, but Berman used the same testimony to show that Matt was a good and fair man who was involved in an awful accident arising out of accepted training procedures.

The third witness on Monday was the senior NCO in charge of twenty-four drill instructors. M. Sgt. Hans Manthey testified that he was going to make Matt a senior drill instructor after this platoon. I questioned Master Sergeant Manthey about the shock-and-fear stage of training, which he said was the shock and fear of coming from civilian life into a completely different life from what they have known. I asked if the training here created a state of shock, and he said it shouldn't have. I then asked:

Question: Did you ever hear of the expression Chief Thumper?
Answer: Well I guess I have sir
Question: Can you tell us what Chief Thumper is?
Answer: Well I have never seen such a man. I have heard there is.
Question: Well you have heard about Chief Thumper. What have you heard about him? Would you describe him to me?
Answer: Well I might say sir that I myself straighten a man's position a recruit's position, and if he...not to do any harm to him at all, just to place his arms in the correct way. Straighten his shoulders, he could I guess tab me...wherever they get that word I don't know.[227]

Master Sergeant Manthey further described that a man might be hunched over and a shove would straighten his shoulders. He denied ever seeing any

---

227 Ibid., 308.

thumping, though he'd heard of it. He also never saw or heard of any night marches except in the papers.

Additional witnesses established chain of custody on the bottle of vodka. Major Holben moved manuals and rules in evidence, including a specific reference to the shock-and-fear stage wherein it was described that prior to training, a recruit "has been treated like a human being by everyone concerned, but the minute he signs his enlistment contract everything changes."

Monday morning started with First Sergeant Hershel Baker, who testified concerning drill training. We asked Sergeant Baker about the definition of discipline within the manual. It said that the "DI does not punish, but may use extra instructions of a constrictive nature. The DI must develop in his men a conviction that is for their good, that it pays off in battle, in having a good cheerful unit and getting their work done quickly and having more time for pleasant things." Then I referred to that portion of the sentence that states that "the DI must develop…" and "may use extra instructions of an instructive nature." I asked, "Would you say that a DI has time to teach his extra instructions?"

> Answer: His time is taken up until 1800 to 1900, as reviewing the day's activity. That leaves from 1900 to 2000 in which time the troops must get a shower, write home, and make the last minute preparations of the day. The only time he could possibly give them extra instructions would be maybe during the weekend, Saturday afternoon, or Sunday afternoon, after church hours.
> Question: And that is when this incident occurred is it not?
> Answer: Yes I believe so.[228]

Whenever a witness gives a lawyer a great answer, it's important to know when to stop. We did just that with Sergeant Baker after that answer. I said, "No more questions."

---

228 Ibid., 305.

The line of questions and answers at this point further illustrated the defense struggle that began here in the inquiry. Had these night marches been conducted by other instructors? Were they impliedly authorized not as a discipline but to teach discipline? Did the manual and rules authorize it? Did they forbid it? Would anyone testify?

Major Holben wrapped his case up with the medical examiner who testified conclusively that the six recruits died of drowning in saltwater. Lieutenant Symthe, Medical Corps, Naval Reserve, testified that the men died of asphyxiation due to drowning, which is based upon the amount of saltwater found in the left chambers of the heart, where it was carried in their blood from their lungs.

Major Holben turned over statements and finished some housekeeping and then closed his case. General Wallace turned to us and said, "The examination of the witnesses called by party are scheduled to commence now." I began:

Counsel for the Party: Well, we have a problem General. I do not know whether you have been made aware of it or not. We have made a request through Major Faw to get immunity for any witnesses whom we would call to testify at this hearing. In this investigation I have been trying to seek witnesses who may come forth to provide or throw some light on the proceedings or the issues this court has before it. We found that the men that might aid in bringing to the court the true facts...that they felt...they were afraid to come forth. They were afraid because they felt if they came and testified and their testimony was in any way critical of the methods used here at Parris Island that their careers as marines would be finished and so they refuse to come and testify because of this fear even though they themselves may not be involved. For example the individual himself would not necessarily have to be guilty of any offense or the breaking of any regulations but he might be an individual who had knowledge that something wrong was going on around the base and even that individual was afraid to come forth to testify and some of these people we talked to told us they would only testify if they got immunity and they got that immunity in writing. Major Faw gave us an answer this afternoon at 1 o'clock. Certain conditions were laid down for granting of this immunity by the Commanding General and we have at this time in our possession the conditions which were laid down by the Commanding General for the granting of this immunity. We will attempt even though we feel these conditions are somewhat stringent and will not be acceptable to these men, we will at least present them what the conditions of the immunity are. If they agree to come in here and testify we will bring them in. So, I would like for that reason and also because we would like to go through these statements to have an adjournment at this time before we decide to call any witnesses.[229]

Gen. Wallace Greene asked us: "How long an adjournment would you like?"

We felt we needed only a few hours. In the five days we had been at Parris Island, we interviewed Marines and tried to get witnesses to testify for the defense about practices such as thumping and night marches. We wanted to show that night marches were not unusual or considered an oppression of troops. But without immunity, no one was likely to come forward.

We communicated to the men we spoke with who may have come forward to testify about night marches and thumping that the conditions of immunity were not guaranteed and not in writing. There were no takers. Thereafter I requested that the conditions of immunity be placed on the record. I have always felt that this is one of the most important things a lawyer can do: simply to say the words "let the record reflect." The court-of-inquiry record reflects that no way was the commanding general of

---

229   Ibid., 327.

Parris Island going to let Marines testify of any widespread problems at Parris Island. At my request, General Greene placed the conditions on the record as such:

> The convening authority has notified the Court that the reasons for not granting blanket immunity are as follows: Blanket immunity might permit someone now under suspicion or investigation to escape punishment. 2. If the party has knowledge of an offense against the code he has a duty to report the matter to proper authorities and if this is done Government Investigators may be able to obtain admissible evidence of the offense, without permitting the guilty person to escape without punishment. However the Convening Authority has stated that he will consider request for immunity under the following circumstances.1. The person for whom the immunity is requested must have been called as a witness. 2. He must have failed to answer a question upon the basis of article 31, Uniform Code of Military Justice. The answer to the question must be material or relevant to the subject of the investigation. 4. The essence of the expected testimony must be conveyed to the Convening Authority and the evidence is not otherwise obtainable.5. The evidence is not otherwise obtainable.[230]

General Greene offered his subpoena power to us. But I answered no. They could be subpoenaed and still would not testify under these circumstances. A subpoena would be useless without immunity.

We had asked to proceed into the night so that Jim and I could get home as soon as possible. We returned to the proceedings at 7:40 p.m. and reported that without a guarantee of immunity in writing we had no witnesses and had only to offer a closing statement. I stood, faced the board, and offered my closing argument.

---

230 Ibid., 329.

If the court please, I will make my remarks standing. Shakespeare once made a statement to the effect—it sounded something like this: "Methinks you protest too much." It seems to me that there is so much proof and evidence that have been produced here to the effect that Staff Sergeant Matthew McKeon was informed about maltreatment that there must be an awful lot of it, else why the necessity of so much warning concerning maltreatment. I would like to begin my remarks by making a request of the court. That request is that General Burger disqualify himself as the officer who will review the recommendations and the evidence provided by this court. We make this request on two grounds. First of all, General Burger, since the date of April 8th, and up to the present has on many occasions expressed judgment of the issues herein. He has, as a matter of fact, and there is conclusive evidence to prove this, pre-judged the issues here. He has, in effect, stated that Staff Sergeant Matthew McKeon is the responsible party and the Marine Corps has no responsibility whatsoever. Now, we submit that General Burger, under these circumstances, cannot possibly fairly judge the issues here. He only could have fairly judged these issues if he had kept an open mind until this Board of Inquiry had concluded its findings and the evidence was presented to him and he read every word of this testimony. He has failed to do this. Another reason or consideration why it might be well for General Burger to disqualify himself is that as a Commander of this post he has the ultimate responsibility for what goes on at this post. He is responsible for every single individual in the United States Marine Corps on this post, and, in a sense, he would be sitting in judgment of himself and it might be a little bit difficult for General Burger to find himself a disinterested party, so I think, if General Burger views the issues that are before him, he might himself voluntarily disqualify himself to judge these issues. Now, concerning the facts of the case, we have had a most unfortunate accident. It is conceded that the troops walked to the water's edge and I believe as far as the actual facts of this accident is concerned the court should take into consideration the fact that Sergeant McKeon was the first one into the water and the last one out. These men who testified here, the survivors, almost to a man have sung his praises, despite the tragic incident which took place on the night of the night of April 8th. That brings us to one of the chief issues of the case. Whether or not there was any maltreatment here. If there was maltreatment, I ask this court, would those men come forward and sing his praises? Major Faw, this evening was discussing an example of maltreatment. He said that there was a case here where some drill instructor ordered a man to run into a wall. Well, that is an example of maltreatment but there is a big difference in that case and the case we have here at hand, because the drill instructor did not run into a wall. In this case Sergeant McKeon was the first one in the water and the last one out, and I feel, in my heart and soul, that if these men followed in the same line that Sergeant McKeon had walked this unfortunate tragedy would not have taken place. Seemingly, from the facts, when they made their turn, some of these men wandered out too far and that is where the trouble began. It might also be well to take into consideration the fact that some of these men, and that goes for Sergeant McKeon and everyone in that platoon, had no knowledge beforehand that these waters were dangerous, and they were not dangerous, they were dangerous because these men did not know their depth. In fact, Colonel McKean, and the record proves it, was of the opinion, despite his 33 months here, that the stream could easily be forded. These men had no knowledge of this current and the testimony is full of evidence that the current these men knew nothing of was one of the responsible factors for pulling these men out into the deep water and causing this terrible tragedy. Now, I am very happy that Major Holben—a great deal was made of the fact that Sergeant McKeon had taken one or two drinks early in the evening—considers drinking not an issue in this case and as a matter of fact the Doctor who was called on to testify here testified that after his examination of Sergeant McKeon shortly after this accident found him to be sober and as far as the Bogan's test was concerned, he just dropped it outside the window and he let the wind blow it away. One more thought on the question of maltreatment. The manual on maltreatment states as the test the drill instructor is to consider, in determining what is maltreatment and what isn't maltreatment, is "If it hurts, it's hurt." In other words to determine, it seems to me, to determine if a punch in the jaw is maltreatment, you should punch yourself first. If it doesn't hurt you then you can go right ahead and punch the recruit in the jaw. That is exactly what that means. There is no other meaning that we can derive from it. The issue here as set forth by Major Holben went: "Where does the responsibility lie?" If there is responsibility, it lies either on the shoulders of Staff Sergeant McKeon, it lies on the shoulders of the United States Marine Corps at this base, or both may be responsible. Or as a fourth alternative, neither one may be responsible for what took place.

Let us consider the first issue, whether or not Staff Sergeant Matthew McKeon has any responsibility for what took place. We submit, that in view that there was no specific prohibition for the use of that area for night training exercises for the teaching of discipline to the troops, that no order was violated by Staff Sergeant Matthew McKeon in what he did the night in question. We further submit, and disagree with the argument of Major Holben, we submit that Sergeant McKeon had authority, both written and implied, for what he did on the evening of April 8th. He had authority in Depot Order 348 to conduct extra activities, to bring out the best in his platoon. There were examples given of what these extra activities should be but these were not all inclusive and Captain Grey, the Company Commander, testified very clearly that the drill instructor is left with a great deal of discretion as far as deciding what these extra activities are to be so that here we have unquestionably in the Standard Operating Procedure of Parris Island, written authority for Staff Sergeant McKeon to do exactly what he did the night in question. As far as implied authority is concerned that is even written more clearly in the facts of this case.

I need only point out to the court Staff Sergeant Huff's testimony here which, perhaps, is one of the key items of testimony that has been offered in this entire trial. We have Staff Sergeant Huff standing before a platoon of men, recruits here at Parris Island, and here we have Sergeant McKeon who is a junior to Sergeant Huff who, perhaps, was standing alongside of Sergeant Huff when Huff said to his men, "If you don't get off your hockey I am going to take you out into the swamps." Here is a superior to Staff Sergeant McKeon telling him, in effect, that this is what we do here. This is how we train our men. Is there any reason then, that Staff Sergeant McKeon, besides this and many other reasons, thought that this was customary procedure here on Parris Island? The conclusion reached on the first issue was that this was not the responsibility in any way whatsoever of Staff Sergeant McKeon. We come now to the issue of the responsibility of the Marine Corps, if it exists. I suggest, along this line, that the court consider the facts that this area, where these men were, was on limits. There is nothing to prove, in this case, that this area was off limits because Captain Patrick himself stated that—it is in the record, that this area was not out of bounds. It was out of bounds only during firing time. There was no specific prohibition by the United States Marine Corps at this base prohibiting the use of that area for training exercises and, as a matter of fact, it was proven here that this base prohibited the use of swamp areas around Elliot's Beach—why did they not make that prohibition a general prohibition to the entire base? Colonel McKean testified there was a rash of exercises in the swamps. That is the exact expression he used. Now, a rash must mean quite a few training exercises in the swamp. It seems to me that this post was on notice of this condition and still they only prohibited the Elliot's Beach area. In law we have a relationship known as a principal-agent relationship and generally the principal is liable for the acts of his agent. The principal is liable for the acts of his agent because he has vested that agent with a certain authority and when that principal—or rather that agent acts in the furtherance of the principal's business, then the principal is liable. There is no getting away from it, and there is no getting away from the fact that the Marine Corps here is the principal and that Staff Sergeant Matthew McKeon was their agent, that Staff Sergeant Matthew McKeon was furthering the best interests of the Marine Corps in trying to teach his men discipline at the time of this unfortunate accident. Now, here we come to the crux of the case and here is a question I am going to put to this court. Are you men going to separate the United States Marine Corps from Staff Sergeant Matthew McKeon? Are you men who created this man, who took him as one of you, who trained him over the course of years, this man who fought in the Korea War under the Marine banner, this man who went to the drill instructor's school here for five weeks, are you suddenly going to disassociate yourself from Staff Sergeant McKeon and out him over on an island all by himself and say, "It is your fault, it is none of ours?" I don't think the Marine Corps is going to do that. I don't think so because I think there is a unity here and if one falls, both must fall and if one stands, I think that both will stand. That brings me to the third point and the final point that I would like to raise here tonight.

As far as this case has been developed, it appears to me that we have here a pure accident. The mere happening of an accident, be it tragic or otherwise, is no proof that some human agency is responsible for it. Now, we have many examples of that. My wife, the very day that this accident happened as a matter of fact, last Sunday, April 8th, she was driving my car and she went through a large puddle and half a block away she applied her brakes, they failed and she ran into another car. Now she might have killed six people when those brakes failed. That was an accident, but certainly no responsibility could be placed upon her shoulders for that accident. She did not reasonably anticipate that the water had destroyed the condition of the brakes. We had another example, recently, of what I call an accident where there was no human responsibility. The case of where Mrs. Woodward shot her husband. A grand jury found that she was not responsible. She made a mistake in judgment. A mistake in judgment is not proof that some human agency caused any tragic circumstances. Here we have a condition where a drill instructor, in good faith, took his men out to teach them discipline. He took his men into an area, not knowing there was any danger there, he went in first himself. If there was any danger there then he would not have gone in first, and he was the last one out. So, this man had no reasonable anticipation of any of the conditions that existed in that swamp area. From all the evidence that has been introduced, it would seem to me, that what we have here is a pure accident. Now, for the Marine Corps, in this instance the officers of this court, to come to that conclusion and to submit such a recommendation, I would say, would require a great deal of courage, because of some public opinion involved, because of some congressmen who have expressed an interest in the proceeding here, but I would like to submit this suggestion. That that would be the determination and conclusion of this body, that they have the courage to make that their determination. I feel that this court and this Corps that has proved itself in battle not to be afraid of foreign enemies such as Japs, Krauts, or Chinese certainly should not be afraid of any segment of public opinion, so I would discount that element of the case. I now would request that this court judge the case on its merits, and I might say that General Greene began the proceedings here asking God to bless these proceedings. I would like to complete my statement at this time with a request that God may give courage to this court to decide this case on its merits. To let the chips fall where they may and I feel that, in all honesty, and in all sincerity, the conviction that the facts of this case call for a determination this was an unfortunate accident and that no human agency was responsible for it. Thank you.[231]

Major Holben offered a rebuttal, and I thanked the court, saying, "Since our arrival here at three o'clock last Friday, we have received the utmost consideration from General Greene and all of the other officers and enlisted men connected with these court proceedings and we are deeply grateful for it."

The court adjourned for the night at 9:40 p.m.[232]

---

231 Ibid., 331–5.
232 Ibid., 331–36.

CHAPTER FIVE

———

THE COURT OF INQUIRY CLOSED for the day at 9:40 p.m. on Monday evening, April 16, 1956. We gathered our papers, packed our transcripts, and said good-bye to Matt. Matt seemed less despondent than when we first arrived. Our work and the support of his family had helped him. I wished to myself, *If only he can keep his spirit up for this long battle ahead.* I feared that the inquiry board would throw the book at him by charging him with some form of homicide, maltreatment of troops, and disobedience of orders. Jim McGarry was optimistic, feeling we had a chance for much lesser charges, if any. He was more confident in our ability to persuade than I was, although I thought we had made strong arguments. I think I spoke for about forty minutes in closing.

We left on that Tuesday morning at 3:45 a.m. Before leaving, I assured Matt he was not in this alone, that we would see him through it no matter what the result the inquiry came to. Matt thanked us again; he could not have been more grateful. Deliberations began the next day but we had to return. Matt's military counsel, Lieutenant Collins, remained present through the deliberations until the inquiry was formally closed on April 18, 1956.

I had known it was the right decision to come to Parris Island, but that night I saw that it was more than that and was relieved we had made that decision to come. I was sure we had helped Matt cross over that threshold of despair to a point where he could begin to see that it was an accident, a terrible tragic accident that all involved would live with forever—one that caused premature death to six young men, but an accident still. As in many accidents, hindsight always provides the clarity that was clouded in the moment by other factors. Oversights are not intentional. Intent is all the difference between a criminal act and a negligent one. That is what I was trying to convey in my closing. There was no crime here, but there was a tragic and fatal accident.

After we left Matt and packed our papers, some of Matt's family waited in the back of the room to speak with us. Ellen, Ned, and Jimmy waited, and once the room emptied, it was just the five of us. I have never seen a family so torn up as Matt's was over this. Seeing Matt in the brig, coupled with the bad press he was getting, had devastated the family. When I told them that last night that I was convinced, utterly convinced, that alcohol had nothing to do with it, his sister Ellen almost fainted and then fell to her knees. Anne's mother, Alice, had tears in her eyes as we spoke, and Jim, her father, silently shook his head, as though what I said confirmed what he knew in his heart—that his boy, his son, would not have been drunk during a night march.

Anne's brother Jim stayed to speak to us further about the possible outcome. Jimmy was pessimistic, and I do not mind telling you that I found it annoying that night. He was critical of Jim McGarry—unjustifiably so. He was preoccupied about the cost of future defense costs if the case went to trial. He did not know how they could possibly afford the best defense counsel. If manslaughter charges resulted, Matt would need the very best. Don't get me wrong: I was confident we had done not only our best in the court of inquiry but as good if not better than anyone else could have done. But I could not do this case alone if manslaughter charges resulted from the inquiry.

I could not answer Jimmy or even give him an estimate what defense costs might be in future. What would be the arrangements? Could I do it? Could I do it alone if I had to? I asked Jimmy to just wait to see what the board of inquiry would do. Could we wait until the decision was in before we worried about cost and before we worried his parents, Alice and Jim, over money they just did not have? Anne's father was retired and lived simply on a pension, and Mrs. McKeon had worked at home raising her eight children, who were all grown. One of her sons was in serious trouble, and she could not do much to help. The inquiry had taken its toll on them.

I said to Jim again, "Let's just wait and see, Jim. We have time to figure it out. After a while there may be some witnesses to come forward about these night marches. We would have had testimony from some if we could have gotten immunity. Matt was acting as others had acted in past. He has many strong defenses, and mostly they lie in the practices of the Corps. Let's just wait and see."

The answer to Jim's worries awaited me in New York City, where a group of lawyers and judges were following the story of the board of inquiry proceedings in the news. A band of New York lawyers and judges wanted to help Sergeant McKeon and wanted to defend the right to a fair trial itself, a right that was being tested by Marine Corps generals who had already publicly condemned Sergeant McKeon before any trial and who were in the position of power that would prematurely decide his fate. I wished I had known that then. I wish I could have told Jim that one of the most esteemed New York lawyers of the day was about to take on Matt's case pro bono. But even when I did tell Jim two weeks later, he was reluctant, and it took some convincing to get him to accept the offer. Jim always took some convincing of what seemed to me to be the most obvious facts. I just had to accept that from Jim, because after Matt, Jim was among Anne's favorites. In sixty-four years of marriage, I have never been quite sure where I fell on that favorites list of Anne's. I think it was an ever-sliding scale, but in 1956, I was running neck and neck in the top positions.

The 3:57 a.m. train from Yemassee to New York City arrived at Penn Station at 7:35 p.m. on Tuesday night. We were home. It was good seeing Anne again. It seemed I had been away from home longer than I actually was. Travel always seems this way to me—I can't get home fast enough. During my nearly week away, I'd missed my daughter Marianne's birthday.

She was five years old. I arrived too late on Tuesday, April 17, to our home on City Island to celebrate my eldest son, Michael's, birthday on that very same day. He was six years old. Anne saved me a piece of his birthday cake and told me about a little cake party they'd had, but mostly she wanted to hear every detail about the inquiry. I told her the parts that were positive. I told her of Matt's defenses. I did not tell her that her mother seemed pale and weak and that the family, especially Ellen and Ned, were taking it very hard or that Matt could go to jail for up to ten years if convicted of an involuntary manslaughter. I did not mention that Jim was concerned about costs and rightfully so in light of the potential charges. There would be time to speak of those things. The night I arrived home I told Anne about my arguments in closing and about the strategy of the defense case. They would not take her brother so easily and lock him up. Then I told her how good it was to be home.

I went into the office on Wednesday, April 18, 1956. It was so much cooler in New York than South Carolina, at least by ten degrees. But I could feel that spring was on its way as I exited the subway to the office. I received two significant calls that day. One call came from Joe Cohen of the *Journal-American*, who interviewed me for an article about the case. More importantly, I received a call from the Honorable James B. M. McNally, justice of the Supreme Court of the State of New York. He had been following the case in the papers and was anxious to form a committee of judges and lawyers to assist in Matt's defense. In anticipation of imminent inquiry findings, we agreed to meet Monday, April 23. This could be the greatest thing for Matt's case. I did not go into any specific details of the case that morning because I did not want to discourage interest. I was really concerned he might cut and run the minute he heard about the booze Matt had had earlier in the day.

Thursday morning at 8:00 a.m., Ned, Jimmy, and Dixie McKeon stopped over at our City Island house on their way home from Parris Island. Anne gave them a big breakfast, but it was not a happy reunion. They were all down in the mouth and terribly depressed about Matt. Mr. and Mrs.

McKeon were obviously stricken, and I had never seen Ned so sad. Anne was maybe the worst of all. The fear of the unknown ahead stilled the air around us. Waiting for charges and the public disgrace of a criminal trial was not nearly as bad as the thought of their brother facing a jail sentence. The idea of Matt in a jail was suffocating to them, and it stilled their spirits to a dread-like fear of breathing, lest the sound of their own life be noticed by the threats they now abided.

On Saturday, April 21, 1956, Lieutenant Collins called me at home to advise that the board of inquiry led by General Greene had recommended that Sergeant McKeon be court-martialed and charged with involuntary manslaughter, maltreatment, and disobedience of orders. As I expected, they charged him with the highest offenses. Anticipating the news of manslaughter charges did not make it any easier to hear. Lieutenant Collins also said that as a finding of fact, the inquiry board found that Matt was under the influence of some alcoholic beverage, but to what degree they could not say. They were hedging. I really felt they had no basis for that finding based on the testimony that there was no clinical evidence of alcohol. This aspect of the case worried me most, as it was the most hurtful piece of evidence, especially in the eyes of the public. Matt would need public support. I was disappointed, of course, and I thought the Marine Corps took the easy way out. It would have been harder for the Marine Corps to admit to a culture wherein these Ribbon Creek marches were more common than they were willing to admit. I was angry, too, that the board made such a finding without an adequate evidentiary basis. The findings awaited review at Marine Corps Headquarters in Washington, which gave us a few days to prepare for its announcement.

My meeting with Judge McNally on Monday, April 23, proved fortuitously timed, as the court-of-inquiry findings awaited final approval of General Burger and General Pate before it was released. I met Judge McNally at 1:00 p.m. in his chambers in the courthouse located at 60 Centre Street in Manhattan. Judge McNally generously commended me on the work we did based upon what he read in the papers. I replied,

"Thanks, but I am not too sure what good it did. I learned this weekend they are going forward with a court-martial on involuntary manslaughter. They also found as a matter of fact that Sergeant McKeon was under the influence of alcohol to some unknown degree."

I worried as I said it…worried Judge McNally would falter in his commitment to form a committee. But to my surprise, he just shrugged his shoulders and said, "So what? 'To an unknown degree' means the same as 'to no degree.' It is extraneous to the issues."

Judge McNally expressed his willingness toward this committee of esteemed lawyers to assist in the defense. He said, "I have already begun contacting some judges and lawyers. Judge Lynch of New York Supreme Court has agreed to join, as well as several other attorneys from different firms in New York. I also spoke with Zuke Berman. You may know him: Emile Zola Berman? Very successful, probably the best trial attorney in the whole city. He holds the record one of the highest verdicts as a plaintiff's counsel. The most recent verdict was three hundred and fifty thousand dollars for a woman involved in an automobile accident. It was a very big verdict because the woman did not work. There was no lost-wage claim involved. I asked Zuke if he would help and serve on this committee with myself and some colleagues, and without skipping a beat, he said, 'Not only would I serve, but I'll try the case.' I was stunned at so generous an offer. Tom, this offer can make all the difference, and he would not charge the McKeon family a thing. There are other lawyers who would serve on the committee, but Zuke would try the case with your assistance."

I was surprised as well and relieved. I told Judge McNally, "I know Berman's reputation well. It would be the answer to the family's prayers and mine because you really need a defense team for a case like this. I am so grateful. Let me talk it over with the McKeon family. I have some cases on the trial calendar this week, and we have a trip planned to Massachusetts this weekend to meet with the McKeons."

We decided to meet again early the next week after my meeting with the McKeon family to discuss Emile Zola Berman's representation.

I knew Emile Zola Berman. Every New York City trial lawyer in 1956 knew him or knew of him. His appearance was unassuming, but he had a keen intelligence balanced by an affability that invited trust. He wasn't tall. He stood a few inches below six feet and was thin and lanky. He wore unassuming wire-rim glasses. His hairline receded beyond his somewhat pointy ears. His eyes were sharp and his look piercing in its focus. He was brilliant, the most brilliant attorney I had ever met then or since. His manner was formal and polite. He was impeccably dressed always in pressed suits and starched, white shirts. When he was on trial, the courthouse buzzed, and lawyers would sit in and watch his trials to learn from him. I was one of those lawyers, and I had seen him on trial in New York County. I wanted him as the lawyer for Matt because I wanted the best for Matt. I had done a good job for Matt, but I was only a few years out of law school, and this was a high-profile criminal case. When it comes to clients, there can be no pride, just loyalty. My loyalty to Matt wanted a seasoned attorney to work his case with. It would just take persuading the folks in Worcester.

When I arrived home from the office on that Monday, I could not wait to tell Anne about Judge McNally and Berman. I ran in the door calling to her. But Michael, my son, answered first with his big news.

"Guess what happened to me," he asked.

I picked him up. "What?"

"Susan Fields kissed me on the nose."

"Like this?" He laughed as I pecked his nose and asked, "What did you do?"

"I did not like that. I pushed her down, and she got right back up and asked me to be her boyfriend."

"She did not!"

"She did, and I said I already have a boyfriend: Ed Rosenberger."

Anne came out from the kitchen and said, "That's right, Michael, and you have a sleepover this weekend as a birthday present. But if you push Susan again, I am afraid all bets are off."

Anne sent Michael off to wash up for dinner and turned to me and said, "I am going to leave him with Marge Rosenberger when we go to Worcester this weekend. Four kids are just too many to take this time."

The seriousness in her demeanor overshadowed her, and even Michael's story had not offered her relief from the burden of those days. I thought it was pretty funny, but I realized then that Anne had not smiled since all this happened. The last time I saw my wife smile and laugh was Saturday night, April 7. We were at the Yorkville Casino on 86th Street for a benefit run for the church at Kilkelly, County Mayo, Ireland. A mob showed up, and over two hundred people were refused admittance. The Costello clan was there: my parents and my three sisters, Teresa, Mary, and Pat, along with her husband, Kenny; my brother, Joe; and Uncle Pete. Anne wore a new red dress that night and looked lovely as she danced to the Irish music and laughed at the stories. Her favorite was always how my father would introduce his sons and, with his thick County Mayo brogue, say how proud he was to have two lawyers for sons. In his brogue, lawyers sounded like liars, and we all got a kick out that. That was two weeks ago. Smiles and red became her. I missed that smile.

"Well, it is, but we will have some good news to tell the family."

She said, "Don't kid, Tom. What could possibly be good news?"

"I met with Judge McNally today."

"What did he say? No go after the news broke about the alcohol?"

"No, he said he was forming the committee with Judge Lynch and some lawyers. One of the lawyers, Emile Zola Berman, the best trial attorney in the city, offered to try the case for free."

"Why would he offer to do it for free?"

It was a good question, but it wasn't one I knew the answer to then. Later in August of that year, after the trial, a reporter from *Life* magazine asked Berman the same question but differently. The reporter asked why Berman, who was making one hundred thousand dollars a year practicing law in New York, would leave his practice to work for three or four months for free. Berman, who was named in honor of Emile Zola's defense of Alfred Dreyfus against the French Army, had read about the McKeon case in the newspapers and believed what was happening to McKeon was shameful.[233] When Emile Zola Berman was approached by Judge McNally, with the memory of his family in his heart, he said yes to the committee and took on a trial that nothing short of destiny called him to.

The court-of-inquiry findings were formally read into the record on Wednesday, April 18, 1956.[234] Thereafter, the findings were forwarded to General Burger, commanding general of Parris Island, for endorsement and action of convening the court-martial. But on April 24, 1956, General Burger added comments that included limited recommendations for change of training tactics, denial of any widespread practices of night marches, and referral to higher authority for action based upon my request that he recuse himself. He wrote: "Counsel for the party raised the question in his argument of the competency of the undersigned to act upon the record of proceedings of the Court of Inquiry...Although I do not consider myself disqualified to convene a court martial to try the charges and specifications appended, I consider that my refraining from doing so will avoid the issue and prevent any breath of suspicion with regard to the trial."[235]

By Monday, April 30, 1956, General Pate, the judge advocate general, and the secretary of the navy all signed their endorsements to the inquiry findings. General Pate added comments to the findings that included the following: "The convening authority approved a recommendation for trial by general court martial and I agree that this is necessary. Accordingly the charges are forwarded for action by the secretary of the navy. The case of Sergeant McKeon is a matter for disposition in accordance with the code, but other matters must be considered. The Marine Corps system of recruit training has been drawn into question. In a very real sense the Marine Corps is on trial for the tragedy at Ribbon Creek just as surely is Sergeant McKeon. I will not blind myself to this fact nor

233 Joe McCarthy, "The Man Who Helped the Sergeant," *Life* (August 13, 1956): 57, 59.
234 McKean, *Ribbon Creek*, 226.
235 Court of Inquiry Findings, General Burger, 16, paragraph 37.

will I seek to disown the responsibility which is mine as Commandant of the Marine Corps."[236]

If I believed that my questions and closing impacted the general's acceptance of some responsibility in this tragedy, I would have been wrong. It was reported later in Colonel McKean's book, *Ribbon Creek*, and reiterated in *U.S. Marine Corps in Crisis* by Keith Fleming that what General Pate feared was a congressional hearing that would expose widespread abuses as evidenced by General Pate's statement:

> "As a result of my statement of the action I am taking, the Committee has decided to hold any further action on their part until we have had a chance to demonstrate that we can set our house in order of our own accord. The Committee has given us ninety days to demonstrate that we can and will do what I have said we will do."[237]

Colonel McKean could not have known at the time, although he suspected according to his memoir, that Major General Twining, commanding general of First Marine Division now housed in peacetime at Camp Pendleton, California, had been called in to assist General Pate in managing the crisis on April 12, 1956. On April 13, 1956, Major General Twining observed stacks of hundreds of manila folders containing thousands of letters from congressmen concerning constituent complaints about recruit training. One such letter reported that a recruit was made to stand on a table and "Proclaim, 'My mother is a whore!'...Those thousands of letters implied a great danger to the Marine Corps. They represented a ticking time bomb that could explode if disturbed by a Congressional investigation."[238]

---

236 McKean, *Ribbon Creek*, 266, quoting General Pate, U.S.Congress, House, Committee on Armed Services, Hearing No. 76, "Report of the Commandant of the Marine Corps," May 1, 1956. *Hearings before the Committee on Armed Services, House of Representatives*, 84th Cong., 2d Sess., 1956.

237 McKean, *Ribbon Creek*, 271, quoting General Pate's post script to policy statement from May 1, 1956.

238 Fleming, *U.S. Marine Corps in Crisis*, 46–47.

General Pate was heading a congressional inquiry off at the pass, and this meant towing a line that the Marines would accept responsibility for change so as not to invite change from Congress. To the extent that General Burger remained steadfast in his approach that this was an isolated incident, his comments were not in accord with General Pate. As a result, General Pate was quoted in the papers as saying that General Burger was transferred from Parris Island for viewing the "case too narrowly as a manslaughter action against one man and failing to recognize also a moral issue involving the whole Corps."[239]

On April 27, 1956, Anne, I, and three of our children drove to Worcester, Massachusetts, where Anne's parents lived. On Saturday, Anne, Jimmy, Ned, and their parents all met at the McKeon house on Maple Tree Lane in Worcester. The house was a side hall colonial with a large living room and dining area to the side of the entry hall. Directly beyond the hall was a family sitting room that was next to the dining room. The last room was a large kitchen. Upstairs were three bedrooms and a second stairway that led to a larger attic bedroom. It was a fine, proud house with china cups displayed in a hallway corner shelf and a dining table that was always highly polished. In the living room, or formal parlor as they thought of it in those days, was a beautiful rosewood-carved player piano that Anne's sister, Ellen, played. There were carved wood settees in Victorian style. We sat in the formal living room, and I laid out our defense theories. I recommended to the family that they accept the services of Emile Zola Berman.

Jim wanted to retain a lawyer recommended by the then senator from Massachusetts, John F. Kennedy. Senator Kennedy recommended a white-glove lawyer from a white-glove firm with a white-glove price. Anne and I pleaded with the family and with Jim in particular (who had influence over family decisions by virtue of his birth order as the eldest son) to accept the offer from Emile Zola Berman. I told Jim that Berman had won the largest jury award to date in New York and was considered

---

239 McKean, *Ribbon Creek*, 268, citing Anthony Leviero, Marine Drinking Linked to Deaths; Shake Up Ordered, *New York Times*, May 2, 1956.

the finest trial attorney in the city. Further, he had the support of some of the biggest firms in New York and many judges on the bench. Finally, he had offered to represent Matt for free because he believed in his case. The attorney recommended by Kennedy would surely bankrupt the family, who had no money to pay for such services. I asked, "Who has that type of money, Jim? Do you?"

I told the family that this offer from Emile Zola Berman to act as trial counsel was more than they had a right to hope for. They were reluctant at first, preferring Senator Kennedy's high-priced recommendation, which they could not afford. Anne convinced them really, not me. They trusted Anne, knew how much she loved Matty, and knew she had his best interests in her heart. Anne and economics convinced them to accept Berman's offer. Looking back, I cannot blame them really. They just wanted the very best for Matt. In the end, that is what they got—they got the best. The McKeon family would accept Emile Zola Berman's offer, and I would assist.

I saw that weekend how brokenhearted Anne's mother was. I felt that she had been called on to carry a great cross in her old days. I began to understand how as a lawyer I would view a case from the analysis of evidence, of testimony, of exhibits, and of expert opinions, but in this cool process was a life deeply involved in the conflict in a way that a lawyer must paradoxically both keep a distance from and embrace to incorporate that human struggle in the communication of a case. The fine balance of analysis and budgeted emotion in a trial presentation was part of the exceptional skill that Berman would bring.

Emile Zola Berman also brought an approach and tone to the defense of Sergeant McKeon that he would be remembered most for. This approach included certain of the elements that we had explored in the court-of-inquiry defense. But Berman's defense strategy captured something we did not capitalize on as fully as Berman did. We made the point that the night march was impliedly authorized and a generally accepted practice. We did this in a somewhat critical fashion. Berman pointed out the same facts, but he pointed them out as a point of deserved pride in Marine Corps tradition.

Since General Pate distanced himself from Marine Corps training practices by promising to correct them in order to satisfy Congress and General Burger had been blind to swamp marches that occurred with a frequency familiar to many a Marine, it invited and opened the door for Emile Zola Berman to do the opposite. It invited Counselor Berman to celebrate the esprit de corps of the US Marines with a view toward confirming that Sergeant McKeon was acting in that proud tradition of training when a panic broke out, causing a tragic accident. This was our defense.

CHAPTER SIX

———

BY THE END OF APRIL, the office I worked at moved to 233 Broadway. Whelan complained about all the reporters calling the office. He told me it had to stop. How was I supposed to stop the press? If I had the secret weapon that would keep reporters away, certainly I would not need to work for Mr. Whelan. The press continued in spite of Whelan's objections.

On the evening of April 30, the nightly news reported that General Pate would appear on Tuesday, May 1, 1956, before a congressional committee investigating the Parris Island tragedy. On this same date, the report from the board of inquiry was under review by the secretary of the navy.[240] The public release of the inquiry findings would coincide with General Pate's testimony before the House Armed Services Committee on May 1, 1956. At the end of General Pate's testimony, Senator Vinson praised General Pate by saying: "During my 42 years in the Congress this is the first time within my memory that the senior officer of any Armed Service has had the courage to state in public session that his service could be deficient in some respect."[241] The Marine Corps was given the opportunity to correct itself.[242] As the Corps accepted its slap on the wrist from Congress, Matt underwent a public whipping largely resulting from the inclusion in the board inquiry findings of an intoxication charge in spite of an absence

---

240 Fleming, *U.S. Marine Corps in Crisis*, 52.
241 Ibid., 53.
242 Ibid.

of any clinical evidence to that effect. That was the finding at the time, and even now I recall vividly that it both enraged and disappointed me most because the medical record showed no clinical evidence of intoxication, such as slurred speech, inability to walk a straight line, and other objective indicia of intoxication.

By the afternoon of Tuesday, May 1, 1956, the inquiry findings were released, and the headlines blasted: "Marine Sergeant Drunk" and "Marine Sergeant on Vodka Party before Death March." As the country read the damning headlines, in New York City Judge McNally began to put together his committee of distinguished lawyers, including Emile Zola Berman. That day I met Berman for the first time in his New York office. He wore wire rim spectacles and a perfectly pressed suit. He was soft spoken and business cool in his expression of both confidence and concern. He introduced me to an associate from his office, Howard Lester. Howard Lester joined the defense team and stayed on the case through the end of trial. The defense team was forming.

The next day, on May 2, 1956, Colonel McKean, commanding officer of weapons battalion on Parris Island, read in the morning papers that he was relieved of his command. The first notice of his relief from command came to him this way, in a morning paper less than three months before his retirement.[243] With this news, Colonel McKean was not going to have the option of walking in slow defiance after a commandant who passed him by in a car decorated with flags specifying rank. Colonel McKean's pride was not wounded—his entire career was wounded. He received a tombstone promotion to brigadier general and under that title left for posterity a now fallen-out-of-print memoir written in a choppy narrative that flips between philosophical beliefs about the Corps and the events of Parris Island as he experienced them in 1956. For years, Anne hid that book—as though by hiding the book, she could hide those very days of our life away—days when some men looked for ways out and others ran in.

---

243 Fleming, *U.S. Marine Corps in Crisis*, 53.

That week I saw Judge McNally in New York County Court. In our discussion of the committee and the defense, I told him how enraged I was at the newspapers' irresponsible handling of the story and equally so at General Pate's statements. I was tempted to make a detailed statement to the press outlining where the reports were blatantly wrong. Judge McNally discouraged it, and only under his orders did I restrain myself. Judge McNally knew that I did not need to make an enemy of the press at this early stage. Members of the press were only doing their job by reporting what was told to them. If I had made an enemy of the press, Zuke would not have been able to gather so much support from them during the trial.

Youth is not an advantage in the law. I was too young and too close to the parties involved: to Anne and her family and to Matt himself. At the time, I thought General Pate's manipulation of the evidence was unjust. His statements to the media that Matt was under the influence of alcohol to an undeterminable degree did not reflect the Marine Corps medical examination that noted the absence of any clinical evidence of alcohol or intoxication and seemed to be designed to deflect criticism from the Corps. Thankfully Judge McNally stopped me from publicly criticizing Pate. At the trial in July, the defense would need and receive General Pate's help in the case, and any public criticism by me would have complicated that effort.

Instead of letters, my May nights were spent researching military law on the rules of court-martial in the New York County Law Library. During the day, I worked on the cases in the office. Zuke began his preparations by clearing his calendar in July and by ordering the transcript of the board of inquiry, which arrived in his New York office in late May.

Zuke found a defense cadence in the transcript of the board of inquiry that another ear would not have heard as clearly. The recruits' testimonial support of their drill sergeant during the court of inquiry created a pattern to Zuke that he replicated at trial by ending every cross-examination of the recruits of Platoon Seventy-One with a series of questions that elicited the same loyalty and support of their drill sergeant as originally offered. Most significantly, the instillation of discipline so integral to the spirit of the corps first mentioned by Lieutenant Collins became the heart of the defense case. Finally, inconsistencies and anecdotes about trout holes and the depth of the creek-bed floor would be clarified by an expert topographer who actually measured the depth of the creek-bed floor. Outside the courtroom, Zuke would be open and generous with reporters, which resulted in a more favorable reporting of the defense position.

On May 8, 1956, Judge McNally publicly announced that Emile Zola Berman had volunteered to represent Staff Sergeant McKeon, with assistance from a defense committee formed and chaired by Judge McNally. The May 14 court-martial date was continued to July 14 at Berman's request. He had cases scheduled through the end of June and would need some time to prepare for this trial.

Judge McNally called every few days to check on the progress. He asked if the charges had been read to Sergeant McKeon, and my answer was yes. Had we received the transcript from Parris Island? Answer: No. Did the records come yet from Parris Island? Answer: No, not yet, Judge, but I heard from Zuke. Zuke is in Florida now, but we spoke on the phone. He expects the records and transcript will come next week. How was Sergeant McKeon's family? Answer: Better, much better. Thank you for asking. They are relieved that Berman has agreed to defend the case on a pro-bono basis. The judge said it was a stroke of luck that he volunteered. Answer: I know—we really are very lucky. Thank you so much for all your help.

The support of the New York Bar gave Anne's family relief, and they all began to feel some relief, almost hopeful—all except Matt's mother, Mrs. McKeon. On Saturday, May 12, 1956, we heard that Alice McKeon had had a stroke and was hospitalized for nearly a week. She almost died. Poor Alice. Her photograph still sits on the marble mantel of this old City Island house that I have shared with Anne for fifty years. The photograph has been there on that mantle for at least twenty-five of those years. In the photograph, Alice is standing next to her husband, Jim. She is wearing a hat and wire-rim glasses. Her white hair is tied neatly in a bun at the back of her neck. Her folded hands are covered in white gloves that stand out against the floral dress that falls to well below her knee and slightly above her ankle. Alice is smiling in the photograph. It is a smile without lipstick or any makeup on her full round face. Her smile is almost shy in its humility, but her head is held with pride in the upward stance of her blue-eyed gaze. Alice was similarly attired in our wedding album. Her dresses were sensible. Her stockings were dark and thick. Her hat and gloves were white. Her light-colored shoes were tied with shoelaces and had a small square heel. She was full figured and matronly in shape in those first days I knew her, as any woman of that age and in that era was who had birthed and raised eight children. Alice changed after 1956.

Less than two weeks after the brutal headlines hit the papers from the court-of-inquiry findings, Alice became ill. She remained critically ill through the summer of 1956. Anne traveled to Worcester on June 23 of that year to be with her mother. She spent two weeks there, returning to New York on July 6. From the date the newspapers excoriated Matt's drinking until July, Alice could not get out of bed. She lost forty pounds in those two months. Later, after her stroke, she developed Parkinson's disease. Thereafter, she would see the world through the confinement of her parlor wherein she sat in an upright, high-back wood chair with curved spindles, covered by a cushion tied to the hard wood with a matching seat cushion. She barely walked, and her few steps were not without assistance. Her voice trembled weakly when she spoke…if she spoke, as she had not much to say but to call the names of her daughters to ask for help. Mostly, she called after Anne's older sister, Mary, who spent her life caring for her parents. Of the eight, Winnie, Mary, Jimmy, Anne, Matty, Ned, Ellen and Francis, it was Mary whose daily care of her parents allowed them to remain in their home all their lives.

After 1956 Alice's once matronly shape fell into her bones. Her muscle disappeared into inactivity, and her head once held upright and slightly back was now bent perpetually forward toward her chest. In later years, her hands shook uncontrollably, her legs would not hold her, swallowing was difficult, and speaking was a struggle. Alice McKeon's heart and body broke in those early days of May 1956. She never wholly recovered, but her faith in God, the Catholic Church, and her family never changed. It was during those days with her mother that Anne developed a lifetime devotion to Saint Therese.

Therese, also known as the Little Flower, was a Carmelite nun who died at age twenty-four of tuberculosis. Before dying, Therese said, "After my death, I will let fall a shower of roses. I will spend my heaven doing good upon earth." Roses then became a sign of intercession by Saint Therese to God. In the summer of 1956, Alice and Anne said the rosary to the Blessed Mother and a novena to Saint Therese for Matty. Alice prayed as she lay on the hospital bed, and Anne prayed on her knees beside her mother. On the last day of their novena, a small boy gave Alice a rose. It was a sign of hope that her prayers for her son would be answered. In the sign of the rose, Alice hoped that Matty would not go to jail and hoped he would find forgiveness. It was a sign that gave us all assurance.

Anne continued in 1956 and ever after to dedicate all her novenas to Therese. She also made other sacrifices for her prayers that summer, including giving up meat. I am a little ashamed to admit that I do not know how she did that, but when we went out to my cousin's wedding in June, I had double portions of prime rib as a result. Anne also gave up coffee, a drink she loved more than any other. I don't know how she did that either. The pungent smell of coffee filled our mornings, settled our dinners, and inspired an awaited energy with flavor and satisfaction. Anne loved coffee, but she made a bargain with God. She was bold that way, bargaining with God, ordering the Marines around, and willing to give up anything or do anything to protect those she loved. Anne told God if Matt was released and found innocent, as she believed he was, she would give up coffee forever. She told God she did not have any more to give up. She could only give up what she loved and hoped he would accept what might appear to him to be a small sacrifice but which to her was significant.

I received double portions of meat, and Anne began drinking tea. I prayed as well, of course. I prayed lots. In my prayers, I prayed for Matty, but I also asked for relief from old-man Whelan. I had received a call from Berman on Tuesday, May 15, that the board of inquiry records had arrived from Parris Island. I received one copy, and Berman had the other. Berman asked me to fly down to Parris Island with him Thursday. I accepted but had not yet asked Whelan for permission to leave. I had a fair idea of his reaction. He would not like it one bit. On Wednesday morning, I attended early Mass and offered Mass and communion in prayer that all would go smoothly for my travels, including permission from my boss. I added a rosary in at my luncheon recess, praying it would go well when I asked him for the time off. It did. He said yes, and I was headed back to Parris Island with Zuke.

On Thursday, May 17, at 8:00 a.m., Zuke and I boarded a National Airlines flight from Idlewild Airport, now known as JFK. It was a new airport then, with the most modern architecture. Ascending from Idlewild in the plane, I could see City Island below us. As the plane circled above the Bronx, it headed south from the base of Manhattan, which appeared as a silvery stretch of spires reaching out to the sunlight. It was and is always a city of reaching. The sun reached back in reflections of light illuminating the concrete, steel, and glass, blessing the aspirations of height touching the sky. We were leaving New York City and heading south to Charleston, a different city of brightly painted, smaller wood structures that predated the Civil War, structures that were spared Sherman's wrath by its surrender and Sherman's own fondness for the place. Charleston was then the closest airport to Parris Island. During the flight, Berman and I read the transcript of the record we received. Zuke was all business. He wasted no time. I was reminded of how precious the gift of his time was. He spent it frugally and productively.

We arrived in Charleston at 11:30 a.m. and were met by Marine Corps defense counsel, Colonel Valentin and Major Debarr. We had lunch in Charleston, followed by a ninety-minute drive to Parris Island that gave us an opportunity to get more acquainted. During the remainder of the day, we met with the Corps's wonderful chaplain, Father Cook. We also met with Major General Litzenberg, the new depot commander. I thought Litzenberg was cold. His demeanor was tough, and his firm square face was unsmiling as Berman reached out to shake his hand. We also met with Major Faw, the law officer who inaccurately predicted internally to the Corps that our defense would be an attack on the Marine Corps, and Colonel Heles, who had presided over the court of inquiry. At the end of the day on Thursday, we met with Matt's wife, Betty.

On Friday, Berman and I met with Matty. Matty had such awfully, awfully sad eyes. I saw the heartbreak in his eyes, and I knew then a certain amount of that would be with him forever. Major Debarr said he thought that Matty was among the great Marines he had met. All counsel—Major Debarr, Colonel Valentin, and Zuke—were 100 percent in support of Matty. Our defense team included Marines I trusted implicitly: Lieutenant Collins, Major Debarr, and Colonel Valentin. Our trip to Parris Island brought the new team of defense counsel to Matty and his wife, and it became not just a case but a man's life.

We left Charleston on Friday evening at 6:30 p.m. and arrived in New York at 10:30 p.m. Anne met us there, as well as Zuke's wife. His wife was beautiful and a real lively gal. My diary reflects that she was a "hot rock," which I confide in you now as I can't get in any trouble now for saying it. We had a drink together in one of the airport lounges. It was the first time I saw Zuke relax in the two days we were together—he had worked the entire time we were away.

Counselor Berman had a hold of the case now. He had read the record, examined the scene, met the client and his family, and conferred with opposing counsel and parties. With Berman at the helm, the defense team applied for Matt's release from jail. That request was denied by the new commanding general at Parris Island, General Litzenberg. Berman set a tone that would continue until after the trial—he appealed. General Litzenberg was overruled by the secretary of the navy, and on May 23,

1956, Matt was released from the brig pending trial. He returned to his home in Port Royal with his wife who was six months pregnant and their two small children. The Marine Corps assigned Matt to the chaplain's office as he awaited trial.

I next heard from Matt in the first week of June when he called Anne and me long distance from Port Royal. He sounded so much better on that call than I had heard in a long time. Here, at last, was a man with some hope. When I first spoke to him on the phone in April, he had been resigned to remorse and did not even want me to come down. When I first saw him in Parris Island during the court of inquiry, he was depressed and in a state of shock. When I next saw him with Berman in May, he was sad and had little hope of getting out of this mess. On June 5 when he called, there was a spark of hope in him that came from being home and surrounded by the support of his family, friends, and lawyers.

The defense team continued to prepare for trial. My job included trying to find witnesses to testify about the frequency of night marches. On the evening of June 7, I addressed the Marine Corps Fathers' Association at the Gramercy Park Hotel concerning whether they would help us gather witnesses for Matty among retired Marines. They fired questions at me about the case, but their attitude was conservative as to how they might help, which was not surprising really given their age. They promised to let me know if they could offer any assistance in locating witnesses. That very day, Colonel Valentin and Major Debarr arrived in New York City. The New York and South Carolina factions of Matt's defense were scheduled to meet on June 8 in New York and review preparations and strategy. Trial was just six weeks away.

On June 8, we started our work after our morning court appearances. Judge McNally, Zuke Berman and his associate Howard Lester, Colonel Valentin, Major Debarr, and I had lunch at the Lawyers Club, then located at 115 Broadway in lower Manhattan. This establishment was the brainchild of a nineteenth-century lawyer who determined there was no decent place to lunch for lawyers in downtown New York. The club consisted of members from the legal and other professions, but it stopped serving after the sixties. By the sixties, stark modernist interiors detracted from the classic gothic ambience of the Lawyers Club. When the Lawyers Club closed its doors, it left a void that has not been filled to this day, as there was no place quite like it in downtown New York then or now.

The Lawyers Club first found its home at 115 Broadway in 1912 after a fire destroyed its original location at the Equitable Building, which is across from 115 Broadway. From 1915 until its close, it was the most impressive of any luncheon club. The Lawyers Club dining room was sixty feet wide, ninety feet long, and twenty-two feet high composing two stories. The focal point of this grand dining room was a floor-to-ceiling stained glass window consisting of fourteen panels of lit glass in two rows of seven. The stained glass panels celebrated the law in a pictorial history that was framed in carved wood gothic spires, which echoed the building's exterior and interior throughout the club. The window is and still remains in the building at 115 Broadway, although now it is in an office that was cut out from the original space.

The window's fourteen vertical panels are centered with two panels in the middle with groups of three panels on each side. The center lower glass depicts a blindfolded Lady Justice with the mayflower above her head, representing the tradition of English jurisprudence that America now practices under. The panel above Lady Justice depicts a tree of several coats of arms, indicating milestones in the law. In this tree, four shields represented the barons who helped win the Magna Carta of English liberties from King John. Among the most cherished and significant of those liberties today, as it ever was, was that no man could be punished except by law of the land. We have to come to cherish this canon of American jurisprudence as "due process" and "equal protection." Other arms depicted in an intricate mosaic of color represent additional milestones of the law, such as the introduction of Roman law to the Normans. The upper three panels to the left depict figures in history, including Emperor Justinian, and advisers who upheld his code. Roman law is depicted below the three Justinian panels, with Darius invoking the law of the Persians and Medes. Ancient Rome and Egypt were symbolized as well. The laws of England were found in the upper panels to the right with pictorials of William the Conqueror. Beneath those were the origins of the laws of England in the Danes and Saxons, and the laws of Normandy.[244]

Other walls of the Lawyers Club were adorned with paintings of great jurists and courthouses of the world, but it was the window that captivated most for its blessing in color, artistic perfection, and inspiration. The stained glass window formed the center of artisan craft within the Lawyers Club, honoring our practice and reminding us that the law is not a recent incarnation or fancy, even if we find ourselves newly anointed to its fold. The law is something more than ourselves or just one case. The law beckons to be kept, cherished, upheld, applied, and above all, respected. I wonder if that is gone now, as gone as the club itself. I resurrect those days in the telling, and I am kept company by those friends and loved ones who have gone by remembering them. In memory, they have returned and are near to me still. In memory, Anne is still here—it is all still here with me.

The stained glass windows of justice in old New York promised the law would find its way as it always historically had: with blind justice, equanimity, and the hope of an abiding progression in the imagination of its practitioners. Sitting below the imposing glass record of the law's significant moments, I, Zuke, Colonel Valentin, and Major Debarr discussed the court-martial of S. Sgt. Matthew McKeon. Colonel Valentin and Major DeBarr had a pressing concern that they believed necessary to immediately bring to our attention. They both expressed their belief in Matt's innocence of the most serious charges and their confidence in our skill and ability to defend him. However, back at Parris Island, Major Faw was predicting a Marine crucifixion by the defense team. Major Debarr said, "Gentlemen, you can understand if we are not able to participate in a defense that is

---

244 Francis Kimball Architect, *The New Lawyers Club of New York City*, G. L. H., Architectural Record, Volume 32 (November 1912), 393–404.

aimed at destroying and criticizing Marine Corps practices. We must respectfully bow out and recuse ourselves if that will be the strategy."

Berman's proud shoulders squared upward, and his military-service-trained back was upright in his chair as he responded: "That is not my intent at all. To the contrary, Colonel, my approach will be to defend the Marine Corps and the very tenet of the esprit de corps. I intend to defend the methods of training recruits, including the exercise of April 8. The Marine Corps is renowned for its battle readiness, and its victories in World War II in the Pacific are legendary. I do not have it in me to forecast a defense that would make any sense by tearing down the Marines. I myself served in World War II. I was an intelligence officer in the air force and served in Burma. I was and today remain grateful to the Marines for their dedication and discipline in battle. No, Colonel, I will not be a wrecking ball to your Corps and its training practices. I will be its defender. The defense of the Corps is the best defense and best hope for Staff Sergeant McKeon, and I intend to give him the best defense."

Colonel Valentin and Major Debarr responded that they would be honored then to serve in the defense with Emile Berman and his team. By God, I felt the same. It was a brilliant strategy.

It was Berman's plan to make the Marine Corps and Matty one and the same so that the judges would be caught on the horns of a dilemma. The dilemma was that if they convicted Matty, they would be convicting and accusing the Marine Corps itself. I believed that his development of the case along these lines would take the Marine Corps by surprise, which it did. I further thought that his praise and respect of the Marine Corps training practices would give Matty a chance, which it did.

I cannot say I could exactly see then how Zuke could pull it off. We were having a terrible time finding witnesses. We had sent out questionnaires to lists of retired Corps men and received no responses. Marines supported Matty but seemed torn and unable to help. Their silence was encouraged by instructions that indicated that they could not be forced to talk to the press and that unauthorized conversations with press might be interpreted as a violation of the Military Code, Article 37, that prohibited "attempts to influence the action of a court martial."[245] This proved a two-edged sword for the Marines, as the gag order gave Berman the sole platform of media attention upon which to launch and reiterate his defense.

For Berman, the defense was not just the trial work in the courtroom; it was a masterfully executed public relations campaign that depicted Matty as a family man, religious man, and dedicated American sergeant. The campaign culminated with a *Life* magazine exclusive interview with Matty and his family after the evidence closed at the court-martial. Berman enhanced media access to the trial in the small details, such as requesting a larger room to accommodate the proceedings, and in the larger details of talking to the press every day and allowing the press access to Matty's family.

The defense was the sum of these parts: executing the evidence and motions with a view beyond prevailing and toward creating a record made by counsel for a viable appeal beyond the verdict. The defense also consisted of building evidence for trial by developing favorable testimony through witness identification and retention of experts. It was assuming the role of counselor in holding up Matty and his wife through the long ordeal ahead, during and after, and in the teamwork of lawyers like myself and Zuke's associate Howard Lester, to assist in locating witnesses, conducting interviews, and researching military law.

In the middle of these days from the end of April until the middle of June 1956, June 4 marked forty days until the trial began. I have spent the better part of my life as a lawyer counting the days and deadlines that define more than beginnings or endings. A lawyer's counting of time compels the tasks that must be completed on a case before a day ends and a deadline passes if not seized. I counted it all: the days and hours of the days and the moments of my life and its obligations to clients, to family, and to church.

As I shared earlier, that year I missed my eldest son, Michael James's, sixth birthday in April of 1956. Anne and I named him after both our

---

245 Fleming, *U.S. Marine Corps in Crisis*, 80.

fathers. I missed my eldest daughter, Marianne's, fifth birthday also in April of 1956. All our three daughters were named after the Blessed Virgin: Marianne, Regina Elizabeth, and Marie Therese, who did not come until 1959. I missed Michael James's kindergarten graduation on May 28, 1956. He reported that his cap fell off when he took a bow and everyone laughed, but we were not there to see it. Anne had to stay home with Tom, my second son, who was sick, and I was working. I count the days I missed as well as the days I did not.

For my church, I began my Legion of Mary work on June 12, 1956, with Frank Mulfeld. Our efforts included visiting a fallen-away Catholic. I do not know if he returned to the church, but Frank and I tried to convince him inside an hour to come back. In that spring a new roof was placed on our Minneford Avenue house, and I trimmed overgrown hedges and grass until the small plot looked, well to me, spectacular. We had fun as well sometimes. Looking over my diary for June of 1956, I see that I played golf and counted respectable scores in respectable courses. Equipped with new Wilson irons, I had a very good game at ninety-two on Saturday, June 23, 1956. On Sunday, June 24, the boys from the Bronx took the boys from Yonkers at Split Rock Golf course and swamped our suburban competitors.

Career counted most of the days of my life in 1956 and would continue to do so until I retired in the late nineties. In late May of 1956, I settled the Shea case for $17,500, representing George Shea as plaintiff's counsel. My share was $3,000, which paid for the roof. I was sent out to jury selection on three other cases and worked to find witnesses in Matt's case, counting the days till trial.

June 18, 1949, Worcester, Massachusetts, wedding of Thomas Costello and Anne McKeon. From left, James McKeon, Alice McKeon, Anne McKeon Costello, Thomas Costello, Mae Costello and Michael Costello (Poppy).

Anne McKeon Costello

CERTIFIED A TRUE COPY:

D. E. HOLBEN
Major, U. S. Marine Corps
Counsel for the Court

COURT EXHIBIT (W)

Court of Inquiry Exhibit 4, Ribbon Creek, April 1956.

Court of Inquiry Exhibit 5, Ribbon Creek, April 1956.

Monday, July 2, 1956
184th day — 182 days follow

Dear Diary,

A letter from Anne arrived today. She describes how her mother made a novena to St. Theresa the Little Flower and on the last day of the novena a little boy gave her a rose. Tears came to my eyes when I read this.

When I recounted it to my sister Theresa she said "Gee I'm hot (the weather is very warm) but that gives me goose pimples"

This augurs well for Matt's future in some manner. I hope that it means complete acquittal.

Mom and Dad took Michael down to Spring Lake, New Jersey for two days. He is really in his element.

Thomas Costello diary entry, Monday, July 2, 1956.
Diary given to me by Thomas Costello.

Thursday, August 2, 1956

215th day — 151 days follow

Dear Diary,
Lt. General Lewis "Chesty" Puller, Marine Corps retired, took the stand this morning and testified for S/Sgt Matt McKeon. It was a very dramatic hour that Chesty dominated in this tension packed court-room. He came out strong for Matt. "What he did was not oppression. A deplorable accident." I am happy to see that General Pate agrees with me that this court-martial should never have been ordered.

Where could you get better testimony. Chesty said to Anne at the N.C.O (Staff) Club tonight "When are they going to release Matt?"

Thomas Costello diary entry, August 2, 1956. Diary given to me by Thomas Costello

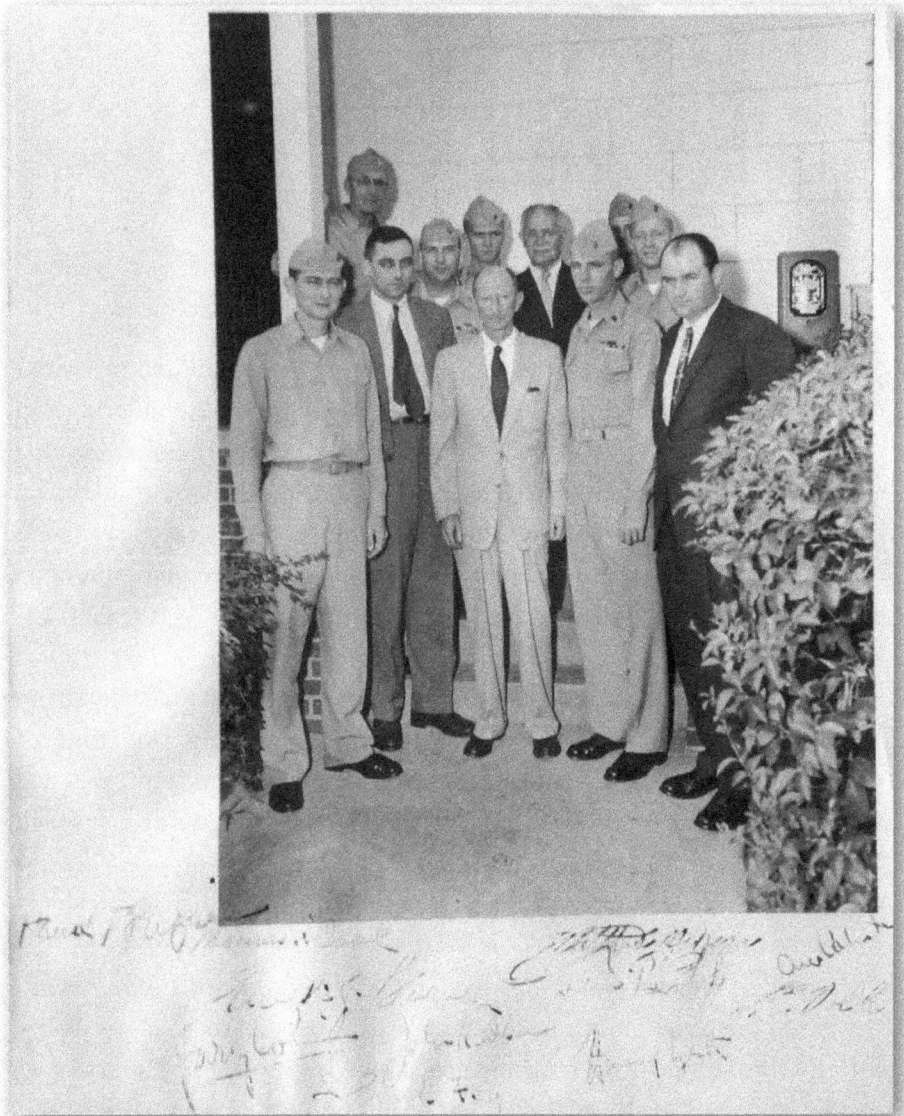

August 1956, photograph of defense team with now faded signatures in the margin.
From the left first row: Lt. Collins, Howard Lester, Emile Zola Berman,
S. Sgt. Matthew McKeon, and Thomas Costello. Standing behind
Emile Zola Berman is Jim Bishop and the Marine Corps defense
counsel. Photograph given to me by Thomas Costello.

CHAPTER SEVEN

———

IN JUNE 1956, ANNE TRAVELED to Worcester with the children to visit her mother and stayed there for a week. This made the house quiet and the nights more restless. I awoke frequently in the middle of those nights alone as though a mysterious interior clock sounded at 3:00 a.m. I think of this hour in the night as a witching hour when the need for sleep is suspended by a race to morning. It is too early to be awake, but sleep will not come. The clock rushes to 4:00 a.m. and then to 5:00 a.m., and then at 6:00 a.m. a sleepless night turns to a tired day.

On one such night, I awoke at 3:00 a.m. after a dream wherein my arms and jaw were paralyzed with the stillness and weight of stone as I stood on the edge of Ribbon Creek. The air was filled with darkness, and the splashing sound of the night water became a faint cry until I could hear Wood's voice pleading, "Get off me! Get off me!" I could see Thomas Hardeman swimming toward the center of the creek. He was swimming toward the sound of splashing. I tried to yell to Matt in the water, "Over there, Matt—over there!" I could not lift my arm. I could not open my mouth to say the words. I needed to scream, "Wood, Wood, Hardeman." My mouth opened slowly to scream, but water entered and began to fill my lungs so that I could not scream and I could not reach out to them. I could only hear them yelling until I heard the sound of water pushing in and pulsing out of my throat. I heard a call, "All good swimmers," and we came. We all came, all of us who could, and it was too late, too late. And then I was awake, the pillow wet with sweat from my neck.

In those sleepless hours in 1956, I often thought of Thomas Hardeman first, a small boy born on October 8, 1935, who stood five feet seven and a half inches tall and weighed 140 pounds. He was twenty years and six months old on the date of his death. His death certificate noted that he had brown hair and brown eyes and a ruddy complexion. He had initially failed the entry test for the Marine Corps, but he kept trying until he was accepted. His brother and stepfather came to Parris Island as the Marine Corps searched for his body. They walked out to the pier where Colonel McKean was overseeing the search efforts. They stood in the cool April air of South Carolina with McKean for over an hour, interrupted only when McKean needed to step away to focus his eyes from tears and clear his throat from the lump that rose to threaten his otherwise stoic stance.

Colonel McKean said that he liked these "plain Georgia country folk." I am certain that he only wanted to help when he discouraged them from viewing the body upon its recovery. He told them the other bodies had evidence of crabs nibbling at them and that this body had been in the water longer and was bound to have more such marks of the creek bed. The autopsy noted the crab damage as avulsion of the ears and nose. Avulsion is a tearing, so avulsion on these young Marines bodies involved crab nibbling and tearing. Colonel McKean told Thomas Hardeman's family, "Don't view the body." He said he would notify them immediately, and he committed to them to working every low tide until Friday at least. Thomas Hardeman's stepfather turned to McKean and said the "the only kind remark" McKean recalled. He said, "May the good Lord be with you and help you, Colonel. We know you are doing everything you can."[246]

There was a call for good swimmers. Hardeman was a good swimmer and answered the call. No one saw him after that, except possibly Grawboski. Thomas Hardeman was laid to rest in Toombs County, Georgia.

---

246 Ibid., 124.

Thomas Hardeman's mother, Magee Meeks, came to the trial and sat in the back of the room. She stared at Matt and at a recess said she hoped he received his judgment on this earth. Matt nearly cried and told her that her son was the finest Marine. Thomas Hardeman had guts, real guts, and that is how Matt would remember him all the days of his life. The memory of Thomas Hardeman may have visited my dreams in those days of 1956, but his life and death stayed with Matt every day of his life. Matt said there was not a day he did not think of those boys.[247]

Norman Alfred Wood's last words were, "Get off me," as he walked in the creek with his arms in the air, simulating what it might be like to be carrying a gun in water. He was six feet and one and half inches tall, with black hair, brown eyes, and a dark complexion, and he weighed 173 pounds. He was the section leader of the platoon who let a tear fall on his dark-skinned cheek when Matt told him he was just like everyone else. Looking back, I think he, like Hardeman, tried so hard that night to be a good Marine and a better man. Norman Wood was laid to rest in Long Island National Cemetery, New York.

Donald Francis O'Shea had blue eyes, brown hair, and a ruddy complexion. He stood approximately five feet eleven inches tall, was 130 pounds, and was born on March 23, 1938. He was seventeen years old at the time of his death. The autopsy report noted contusions over the left zygoma and abrasions about his eyebrow, possibly the result of fighting in the water, a fight he lost. He was laid to rest in Middlesex County, Connecticut.

Charles Francis Reilly weighed approximately 143 pounds and stood five feet nine inches tall. He also had blue eyes, brown hair, and a ruddy complexion. The autopsy report noted that his eyelids and upper lip had multiple lacerations. He was laid to rest in Cayuga County, New York.

Leroy Thompson was born on November 21, 1937, in Summerton, South Carolina. He had relocated to New York but died in the state of his birth at age eighteen and four months. His eyes were brown, his hair was black, and his skin was dark. He weighed 170 pounds and stood

---

247 *Boston Globe*, January 7, 1990.

approximately six feet one inches tall. He was laid to rest in Greenville County, South Carolina.

Jerry Lamonte Thomas was born in Columbia, South Carolina. He was five feet six inches tall, 129 pounds, and seventeen years and four months old. He was laid to rest in Arlington National Cemetery, Virginia.

I knew these young men only by their death certificates and through the testimony of their platoon mates. The record of their lives rests in the drape of the American flag that covered their coffins and covers the coffins still of the fallen and of those who served in the past. They share the mark of having strived for something sacred not reached. The reasons for this tragedy are many. Our work in the trial was to place a light in the dark corners of some of those reasons, but it was not without the deepest reverence and sorrow for these prematurely perished lives. Their memory has not left me, nor my family. There was not a spring that came to us that Anne did not pray in gratitude for God's graces and in hope for his forgiveness for all our failings in those days in 1956. She prayed not just for those failings of her brother, because he was not alone in committing grave errors. It was shared by many.

Sometimes from the night quiet of a dream's disturbance, their death would visit me where I could hear, but not see. I could breathe, but not air. The cadence of repeated prayers would not chase their images away. Still I prayed for them and for us who they left behind, and there was some comfort in the repetitious pattern of saying the Hail Mary and Our Father. If I had those nights, and I did, how many had Matt had? Did they ever leave him? I think not. How many nights like these did Anne have, or the families of the deceased Marine recruits, or the Marines of Platoon Seventy-One, or of Alice and Jim? All these lives were touched, some broken and others lost, by the seemingly fleeting moments of mistakes in judgment that turn a life forever and leave an eternal mark on time.

Matt told a reporter years after this tragedy that he thought of those young men every day of his life. He thought of where they might be in their life, who they may have married, what children might they have had.

At the end of his life, he said he had lived a good life, except for that one time, that one mistake. But Matt had taken responsibility here on this earth. Matt had been brave as a young man on the *Essex* and throughout his service. He was brave during his trial. He was brave in his life and brave in his death. For Matt, I believe if his days had remorse, his nights had the comfort of prayer, and in his life after death, he found forgiveness.

In my life, I have prayed in the morning hours for forgiveness for my mistakes, and at night I dream still of forgiveness failing. I dream of loss. I dream of imprisonment. I dream of days of deep drunkenness when I did not recognize the lines of my face or the path of my own life and beliefs. I dream of mistakes that cannot be unmade, of what I should not have done but did anyway and what I could have done but did not do. I dream of Anne. I dream and hope when my days are done, there is someone to come get me and accompany me to the place where my spirit may find its home and my body find its rest.

CHAPTER EIGHT

———

FOLLOWING A RESTLESS NIGHT, ON Monday morning, June 25, 1956, Zuke called. He wanted to meet for dinner. We arranged to meet at Keens Steakhouse at 72 West 36th Street. I had never eaten there before but had heard so much about it that I began to look forward to an evening out and away from the empty house. Keens was and still is one of the oldest steakhouses in New York City. Unlike the Lawyers Club, it is still there today. It is still as opulent now with its dimly lit art-filled walls and steak-laden plates as it was then. It is also as eccentric and legendary now as it was then with its ceiling adorned with rows of long antique smoking pipes.

The day dragged as I looked for things to do to fill a day of billing in Whelan's office until five o'clock came. I took the 2/3 train to 34th Street and walked a short distance to Keens Steakhouse on 36th. Zuke was waiting at a table in a corner with a silver-haired, distinguished-looking gentleman who was a journalist with the Hearst papers. Jim Bishop had become a well-known and extremely popular writer with the publication of a book in 1954, *The Day Lincoln Was Shot*. In 1956, he was a syndicated columnist with the Hearst papers and could cover any topic or special assignment of his choosing. The McKeon trial was Jim's current assignment of choice, and his writing would reach millions of readers. Jim planned to begin his work by traveling to Worcester to gather background information from Matt's family and friends. I (along with Anne) ultimately introduced Bishop to the McKeon family and friends.

Bishop's columns offered a more human portrait of the drill sergeant. Under his signature in 1956 of "Special Writer, Hearst Newspapers," Jim Bishop wrote plainly, albeit forcefully, about Matt's life beyond the waters of Parris Island and about the trial. The articles appeared in over two hundred newspapers nationwide. Berman gave Bishop open access to Matt, and Anne gave Bishop open access to the entire family by driving him around Worcester and introducing him to friends, family, teachers, and neighbors, all of whom he interviewed and all of which he wrote copiously about every week until the verdict, reaching the homes and hearts of literally millions of Americans. The Marine Corps, on the other hand, put a gag order on its members.

Bishop's columns described April 8, 1956, in detail. Many of his columns, including those of the court-martial, are collected in a book entitled *Jim Bishop: Reporter*, by Jim Bishop and published by Random House in 1966. Bishop's columns described the task of "making Marines from boys in seventy days," after which a Marine is born who must be "clean, healthy, know that his best friend is his rifle; he must be sure that, in battle, the man on his left and the one on his right will not break and run…to do this the D.I. must be tough. The commissioned officers have little to do with the matter. They rank the D.I., and they supervise, but the vertebrae and marrow of the corps is the drill instructor."[248] Using Matt's own words that in Korea he was happy to know the men beside him would not cut and run, Bishop in his columns offered the public Matt's motivation in conducting the march.[249]

Matt wanted to build in the staying grit of men who would not cut and run. Matt knew from the experience in World War II and Korea that wars are not won by one man with courage. Rather wars are won and men of war survive by a team of courageous unafraid men in groups of thirteen, a squad; in forty or more, a platoon; in two hundred, a company; in a thousand, a battalion; in three or more battalions, a regiment or brigade;

---

248 Bishop, *Jim Bishop: Reporter* (New York: Random House, 1966), 115–16.
249 Bishop, *Jim Bishop: Reporter*, 116–18.

in three or more regiments, a division; in three or more divisions, a corps; and in three or more corps, an army. But the Marines Corps was more than all of this: the Marines are the "elite fighting outfit of the world."[250] In seventy days, a drill instructor did not make men from boys but made Marines from men.

Bishop described Anne's brothers and sisters. Bishop's description of Alice was heartbreaking and painfully honest. He told the story of how a reporter came to Alice McKeon's door on Monday, April 9, 1956, and asked for a photo of Matt because there was an accident on Parris Island and he was the only survivor. He told of how Alice gave him a photo. Alice was so thankful that her son survived and told her family that it was due to the extra prayers she said on her knees every night for her son because he was still in the service. Then, the evening paper delivered to her door reported: "Tipsy Sergeant Drowns Six Recruits " with the very photo she had given the reporter. Bishop reported: "Alice McKeon was in the hospital the next day with an oxygen mask over her face. Her heart was involved in more ways than one."[251]

"*Jim Bishop, Reporter,*" as he was known in his columns and in his book of the same name, was one of the miracles of faith that occurred in the days immediately preceding Matt's court-martial. Alice's prayers were not in vain. A country divided in opinion over a hotly debated case and a Marine Corps generally united in opinion that Corps training was becoming too soft, found in Bishop's columns the nuanced details of all sides of a tragedy. These details did not diminish the Marines who died, not at all. Rather, Bishop's detailed description of April 8, 1956, included clear images of the following tragic fact: "Six boots, given in trust by parents to the United States Government, floated beneath the surface, their faces in repose, hair lifting and falling, as they made slow time to the sea."[252] It is an image that still haunts me.

---

250 Ibid., 127.
251 Ibid., 129.
252 Ibid., 125.

Bishop was an Irish Catholic reporter from New Jersey who wrote for the New York papers early in his career. His style of writing emulated his personal hero, Hemmingway. His writing echoed an unapologetic directness common to New York City, where he learned his craft as a master wordsmith. Bishop's background gave him insight in his writing as he described Matt's days in Parris Island awaiting trial. During that time period, Matt was assigned to assist the chaplain, Father Cook. He assisted at mass and drove Father Cook to the infirmary to visit the sick. Matt's nights were spent with his wife, five-year-old daughter, and ten-month-old son. Bishop juxtaposed the sound of Marines who said of Matt, "Poor Mack," against Matt's own words that acknowledged his responsibility. Bishop gave the American public the Marine Corps heart that remained in the man they condemned and restored Matt's identity to himself. The public could not help but to feel sympathy for Matt after reading Bishop's columns.

As public opinion softened, the defense worked harder and faster as trial approached to locate witnesses to assist in the defense. To this task, our effort continued throughout the preparations and the trial. On Friday, June 29, 1956, I had lunch at Miller's New York with Jim McGarry and United States Marine Corps Major Doyle (who was set to retire the very day after our lunch). Our conversation was interesting, and I learned that Major Doyle hoped to publish a book entitled *One Was a Marine*. But Major Doyle did not offer any direct help for Matty, and our search for Marine witnesses continued.

On Saturday, June 30, just two weeks before trial, I traveled to Utica, New York, to speak to the State Convention of the Marine Corps League of New York. I was scheduled to speak in the afternoon, but my speech was moved to the evening banquet. My speech there on behalf of Matty was the best received of any I gave. After my speech that evening, I was welcomed by the many Marines in attendance and felt the genuine swell of support for Matt, perhaps invoked in part by what I had said. Still, we had no witnesses come forward. If only the Marines who had almost unanimously raised their hands to show Colonel McKean that they too had been participants in night marches along the creeks and marshes of Ribbon Creek had come forward. They did not and with good reason.

Bishop called it a gag order in the title of his July 17 column: "Officers Gagged on McKeon Aid by Parris Brass."[253] Bishop was referring to an admonition from Marine Corps headquarters dated July 11 that read: "Article 37 UCMJ. Any unauthorized conversations with reporters could be a violation of Uniform Code of Military Justice, Article 37, which prohibits attempts to influence the action of a court martial."[254] The Marines had been warned. They had been threatened. They were silent, mostly, but not entirely and not for long. The next week brought me from New Jersey to Massachusetts looking for witnesses. In the swiftly moving weeks to come, witnesses would begin to look for us.

The Marine Corps did not expect a unified defense from so many fronts. It left them baffled. To this day even, different people offer various reasons for this. One oral history of Marine Corps brass speculated that Matt's large Catholic family had ties to Cardinal Spellman, the sixth archbishop of New York from 1939 to 1967. Another book said we had a relative who was a judge and that he asked Berman to help. No, we had no relatives of power I knew of, and Berman volunteered without being asked. It was not family or religion or Cardinal Spellman who motivated our team of lawyers that consisted of more non-Catholics than Catholics. It was our respective, albeit diverse, heritage that hailed from other countries to this, our staying place that promised equal opportunity, equal protection, and equal justice.

---

253 Jim Bishop, *New York Journal-American*, July 17, 1956.

254 Fleming, *U.S. Marine Corps in Crisis*, 80.

——

CHAPTER NINE

ON JULY 9, 1956, A new convening order was issued that appointed three additional judges to the panel that would preside over the court-martial of S. Sgt. Matthew McKeon. The members of the panel were Col. Edward Leigh Hutchinson, Lt. Col. Nicholas August Sisak, Lt. Col. Duane Fultz, Lt. Col. Daniel Joseph Regan, Maj. Edwin Thomas Carlton, Maj. John Gust Demas, and Lt. (Navy Medical Corps) Bentley A. Nelson. Capt. Irving Klein, US Navy, served as the law officer, a position similar to a judge of law and responsible for rulings and presiding over the proceedings. The courtroom was an auditorium of the depot children's school, which was not equipped with a sound system.

At the pretrial conference held on the Friday before trial was to commence, July 13, Berman asked the law officer for microphones. He said the acoustics were so poor that "members of the court may have to lean out of their chairs and Counsel hover over a witness while he is talking to hear. It is going to make it very uncomfortable. I am sure they must have some kind of system here where they can set up mikes by these witnesses and for the various participants. You would only need one at the counsel table, one at ours, and one at the witness, and perhaps one for the Law Officer."[255]

The prosecutor, Servier, was not opposed to the installation of microphones, nor was the law officer, but Major Faw expressed reservations. He indicated that no effort has been made to produce microphones to

---

255   Trial Transcript, Appellate Exhibit 9, 10.

broadcast the hearings to spectators and said, "My first concern is that I know of no such equipment at this depot—it took me seven months to obtain a conference microphone so that we could record what went on with a conference machine....It may be that a microphone system could be set up but at the moment I don't know of it. My second concern is that I have never been in a courtroom anywhere at any time where a microphone was used. It is a completely novel impression to me. I would like to think about that myself."[256]

Captain Klein asked Major Faw if microphones had been used in hearings, and he acquiesced. Captain Klein next asked Berman if he knew of the use of microphones in courtrooms, and Berman said, "They have been used in courtrooms throughout the States, Captain."[257] By the second day of trial, a microphone system was installed. But there was no air conditioning in the auditorium. The Spartan room had sound and seats, but it was not a room of the caliber of courtrooms in usual practice, even for those days.

As the pretrial conference proceeded in Parris Island, I was in New York City wrapping up my week of searching for witnesses who would be willing to testify and confirm what we believed and what we knew to be true: that the night marches of the sort conducted on April 8 had occurred in the past on Parris Island and not infrequently. On Wednesday, July 11, 1956, Tom Geraci, a retired Marine, mailed me a list of about three hundred former Marines in the metropolitan area. I set up a committee of lawyers in New York to contact the Marines on the list to ascertain if they had anything of interest and value to the defense. Joseph Costello (my brother who is also a lawyer), Tom Cronin, Jim McGarry, John Conner, Dorn Pelli, John Cortis, Joe Muldoon, and Vinny Scalfani all made phone calls on behalf of Matt's defense. The race was on to locate witnesses.

From downtown New York, phone calls from our New York committee of lawyers reached out to retired Marine Corps in the New York

---

256 Ibid., 12.

257 Ibid., 13.

metropolitan area and beyond, even as far as Virginia where retired Lt. Gen. Lewis B. Puller lived. Our work, and that of lead counsel Berman, had also reached as far as Washington, and it would reach a national audience before it was finished.

Berman sent letters to the secretary of the navy in Washington requesting that the defense be allowed to review and examine the questionnaires that General Pate had sent to Marines seeking their commentary on the training of the Marine Corps. Berman also asked the secretary of the navy for a list of Marines discharged from Parris Island that year. The secretary of the navy deferred the decision of the release of the questionnaires and lists to the presiding court-martial Law Officer Klein. If Captain Klein refused access, it provided grounds for appeal. If Captain Klein assented, Berman would certainly find the same evidence that Colonel McKean found when he asked Marines in April on the dock overlooking Ribbon Creek if they had participated in swamp marches. According to McKean's memoir, they had in fact been made to march in like manner, so much so that one of the men, Staff Sergeant Fortner, said "he had that experience virtually every night."[258] Berman's request for names and the questionnaires was the beginning of developing a record sufficient to provide a foundation for appeal.

Berman arrived at Parris Island for trial on Thursday, July 12, 1956, with a young associate, Howard Lester, and a second young lawyer, Mort Janklow. Mort would not stay for the duration of the trial, as his motivation to obtain the rights to Matthew McKeon's story brought an invitation to leave the trial midway, but that would not come until week three.

In that first week, I was still in New York conducting potential witness interviews. In Newark, New Jersey, we interviewed a potential Marine Corps witness, Billy Cortes. We signed him up with the certainty that he would be helpful to us. I regretted not getting the list of retired Marine Corps earlier but was so grateful to have received it at all. We hoped to find

---

258 McKean, *Ribbon Creek*, 229–30.

at least twenty good witnesses out of this group. I thought at the time that if we could get that, then we would be fine.

I traveled to Worcester in search of more witnesses, and Berman was in the pretrial conference on Parris Island on July 13. At the pretrial conference, Berman offered to enter a stipulation in the record that the cause of death of the six recruits was drowning. His stipulation should have made the necessity of evidence regarding the cause of death unnecessary. That evidence consisted of both the death certificates and photographs of the deceased recruits, the latter which Berman objected to being included in the record of evidence. Berman would renew this very objection at trial concerning the entry of the photographs. He argued, albeit to deaf ears, that the photos offered nothing probative, particularly since he had stipulated to the cause of death. During trial he argued this point first raised at the pretrial in the following objection:

> Mr. Law Officer, I respectfully invite your attention to the fact that under the terms of the charges and specifications the incident which formed the basis of the charge of criminality occurred on or about 2030 hours on the evening of 8 April, 1956. As I understand the testimony of this witness, this proffered exhibit had its origin at forty three hours thereafter during which these specifications were typed and I ask you take judicial notice of these forty three hours variation and with respect to this I urge it is prejudicial and is not a fair representation of the deceased except the remains and there is no admission of identity and the whole purpose of flooding this record with exhibits at this time is inflammatory…I make the same objection as I previously made with respect to all the exhibits and specifically to the one proffered exhibit concerning rigor mortis. I specifically and respectfully invite the law officer's attention to the exhibit and trust it will be excluded from the record.[259]

---

259 Trial Transcript, 96.

The law officer rejected his plea in a one-word response, "Admitted," thereby ruling the photographs would be admitted in evidence at the time of trial.

At the pretrial conference, Berman moved on to his second motion: to separate the alcohol charges from the other more serious charges. Berman supported this request with case law and the rather minor result of the charge against King and Scarborough. As there was no evidence of intoxication, Berman argued that the inclusion of the minor charges tainted the process. That motion was also denied. Their last business in Parris Island that day was the logistics of the room and need for a sound system, the only acquiescence Berman achieved.

As Parris Island closed its conference on Friday, Jim McGarry and I left 120 Broadway, New York, at 4:30 p.m. to drive to Worcester to meet with Marine witnesses. The traffic to Worcester was horrendous, and what should have been a three-hour trip took five hours. We arrived at the home of Alice and Jim McKeon on Maple Tree Lane in Worcester at 10:30 p.m. Their modest Victorian-style parlor was filled with at least nine Marines waiting for us. Alice was more frail than I imagined and much weaker than I thought. When we spoke, she said in a weakened whisper: "It's such good news that so many men, so many Marines want to help Matty."

I tried to lift her spirits more by saying, "Matt has the very best lawyers in New York working for him. I hope you saw some of the articles by Jim Bishop. We are working very hard, Alice, and I don't want you to worry."

That night we set to the ongoing work of interviewing those men who had waited so patiently for our arrival. We sat at the dining-room table taking notes of their experiences in training. We signed up six Marines as definite witnesses. It was a valuable night's work, followed by more interviews the next day.

On Saturday morning, Jim McGarry went out and saw two former Marines around Lawrence, while Matt's brother Ned and I toured Worcester. In all we gained four additional witnesses of fairly good caliber.

At 4:00 p.m. on Saturday, July 14, we left Worcester and drove south toward New York, arriving at our friend Tom Cronin's place in Stamford around 7:00 p.m. Tom gave us dinner and drinks and reviewed our progress at putting together witnesses concerning the practice of night marches. We gathered more evidence for the defense in Stamford by adding Larry Turner, a former drill instructor who would make a very favorable witness. I left Stamford a little before 10:00 p.m. and got back to City Island around 11:00 p.m. Anne had my bags packed and ready to go for departure to Parris Island in the morning. Anne planned to travel to Worcester to be with her mother for the beginning of the trial. She would not join us in Parris Island until midway through the trial on July 24th. The defense was as well situated as we could have hoped for. I had traveled from New England to the South in search of Marine Corps witnesses, and while we had found many, there were more still to come.

On Sunday morning, I just missed the 8:00 a.m. flight out of Idlewild by a few minutes, but I was able to get the 12:45 p.m. flight, which took seven hours. It was a milk plane that made all the small stops on the way down and required repairs as well. After arriving in Charleston, I went directly to Father Cook's house where Matt was assigned pending trial. Jim Bishop, Burris Jenkins (who was the *Journal's* illustrator), Father Bielski; Father Flaherty; Matt's brother Jim; two of his sisters, Ellen and Mary; and his wife, Betty, were all there. Matt sat in the midst of his family, his spiritual advisers, and his counselor, Zuke Berman. Matt was glad to see me, as was Zuke, who put me right to work at the BOQ where all the behind-the-scene trial preparation was happening. There was so much activity and papers flying, calls being answered, and notes being taken, that I was dumbfounded by it all. Our team was split up by tasks and had been working different angles. Howard Lester, a brilliant associate of Berman's, had been concentrating on legal research. I was concentrating on witness location. Zuke was coordinating the entire effort—which beyond preparing questions included a masterful public relations effort that gave open access to the defendant and the defense.

The first day of trial, Monday, July 16, 1956, was hot and sunny. The court-martial of S. Sgt. Matthew McKeon convened with introductions in a crowded auditorium that still awaited installation of the much-sought-after sound system. The counsel for the defense did not remove his jacket in spite of the sweltering heat unabated by fans. He stood up and began by saying simply, "Mr. President, Officers of the Court, my name is Berman, Emile Z. Berman."

Berman's opening questions for *voir dire* of the judges did not shrink humbly behind the difficulties anticipated ahead. Rather he used the anticipated weaknesses of the case as vignettes that sealed a promise of fairness from the judges. He said, "I want to make it plain to you that it is neither my function nor my desire to cross-examine you, if I may use that word. So I hope none of you get that impression."[260] Berman then questioned each of the seven judges about the most controversial inflammatory pieces of the trial. He addressed intoxication, bad press, and chain of command on the evidence. At the end of his questions, he solicited from each judge a promise and commitment to be fair.

I have always believed *voir dire* to be among the most significant parts of a trial, as it is the only part of a trial where counsel and jurors speak together in conversation and get to know one another. It is the part of a trial wherein a defense attorney can try to communicate to the fact finders—be they jurors or judges, as in this case—that at the end of the day, the defense attorney must return to a client and say honestly that he or she did his or her very best to secure a fair panel and each promised to be fair to each party.

Berman's *voir dire* fulfilled that obligation. He asked the judges: "Do you as a matter of your concepts equate the taking of a few drinks with intoxication or drunkenness?" He asked:

Without asking you gentlemen specifically the nature of these stories which you read, and I might as well be brutally frank about those headlines in the early days, captions all over the country

---

260 Ibid., 10.

about "Drunk leads death march." The newspapers have their own ways of phrasing headlines, I say this in the presence of a large body of press here. My question to you Colonel, is, and it is only for you to say, I am sure that you know yourself, I have only had the pleasure of a casual meeting with you, but upon examination of yourself and what it has taken of your life to make you what you are today, is there the slightest doubt, should I for example, who bears the weight of the responsibility of the defense for this sergeant, have the slightest concern that in any wise, headlines of any kind recent or early will interfere with your judgment in this matter?[261]

Berman continued, "In other words, whatever it is you have read and whatever is even if you may recall, now what you have read so far as this trial is concerned, and the fundamental rights both of the government and of this sergeant your views will be taken from the evidence and your view of the truth and the probabilities of this case." Berman not only solicited a promise of fairness to his client but to the opposing side as well. While this may appear counterintuitive, in *voir dire* it enhances counsel's credibility before the fact finders and illustrates that in his advocacy that the pursuit of a fair trial for his client is paramount. The promise to be fair to both sides and the commitment to base a decision only on the evidence to be presented—not news reports, not speculation, not gossip around the base, but the evidence alone—is a foundation of what a lawyer must achieve. Getting fair jurors is the goal of *voir dire*, and no one did it better in 1956 than Berman.

The defense also directly faced the General Pate problem in *voir dire*. General Pate was the commandant of the Marine Corps. As such, it would be easy enough to disregard his statements if you are a citizen, such as myself, or even as a former army private. As a veteran and citizen, General Pate was not my commandant, but he was the judges' commandant. Berman did not avoid the dilemma that General Pate's earlier public condemnation

---

261 Ibid., 12.

of Matt wrought. The panel consisted of General Pate's very subordinates, who were now called upon to sit in judgment of Matt. How could they be fair? How could they disregard their commandant's comments?

Berman went directly into the issue of the impact General Pate's statements may have had on the judges by asking:

On May 1st in 1956, the Commandant of the Marine Corps, General Pate, testified publicly before a committee of a house of Congress, called the Armed Services Committee. That testimony, coming from a man of such high status, properly was fairly widely distributed and fairly widely covered by the press from one end of the country to the other…in that case I will ask you pointedly sir, whatever your recollection is, vivid or dim, and only you know, what recollection you have if at all, do I have your assurance that whatever that recollection is as to what the Commanding General of the United States Marine Corps testified to will play no part in your deliberation and decisions in this case?[262]

Imagine the difficulties required of the Marine Corps judges promising to disregard their commandant or of a Marine Corps defense requiring that promise. It also clarifies why Berman called General Pate to the stand on the defense case at trial. The defense entered the trial with the condemnation of an elite Corps leadership, an expert topographer to testify that there was no sudden drop in the creek, and retired Marines willing to testify that the marches occurred during their training as well. But there was little else when the trial started.

On the second day of trial, Tuesday, July 17, 1956, Berman felt he was short on evidence of the past practices of night marches despite our efforts. He had met his responsibilities as defense counsel, but he knew he needed more evidence. Honoring obligations was not enough. So Berman

---

262 Ibid., 14, 15.

took a calculated risk. On Tuesday, July 17, 1956, the court adjourned at two in the afternoon to allow for the installation of the sound system. The afternoon break in the proceedings gave Berman an opportunity to make a public plea for assistance. Berman went on national television and appealed to the national newspapers for all former active Marines who have knowledge of training methods at Parris Island to call him collect.

The calls began coming in around 5:00 p.m. that evening, and once it started, there was absolutely no stopping it. The calls flooded in, one after another, from every corner of the country: former Marines volunteering to come to Parris Island and testify for the defense regarding their experience at Parris Island with night marches. Parris Island in all its history had never seen anything like this, and I in all my fifty-plus years of practice never saw anything like the response by Marine Corps veterans from every State of the Union. It was a small miracle to get so many phone calls, and our defense case began to build momentum.

That night the defense team conferred with hope and a late dinner at the Golden Eagle Tavern and Inn in Beaufort, South Carolina, main side from Parris Island. I recall vividly drinking, eating, and discussing the number and quality of calls as we overlooked the waterway between Beaufort and Parris Island. The inn had a garden entry of palmettos and magnolias that departed from the austerity at Parris Island. The old inn is now long gone, but I remember it provided the homespun comfort of an excellent dinner served in plain elegance of freshly pressed linen tablecloths surrounded by antique china cabinets filled with crystal. Berman, Lester, Bishop, DeBarr, myself, and Valentin sat at a corner table near an open window that offered cool night air, and we discussed the calls coming in and how to sift through them. We decided that night that we would take all Marine callers who had marched in any type of mud or swamp.

The next day, volunteers took calls, and the trial continued with opening arguments. The prosecutor offered brief opening remarks consisting of approximately one paragraph. Law Officer Klein then inquired, "Does the defense desire to make an opening statement at this time?" Berman rose and said the defense did. Looking at the transcript now, Berman proceeded for what is recorded as six pages in single-space lines. I watched as Berman opened, adhering to the simple yet singularly significant overview that answered the questions for this jury of Marine Corps judges. He told them who Matt was, what had happened and where (concerning the evidence of the creek bed), and when and how it happened. Berman punctuated these questions with a dignity and honesty that set the tone for this trial. He first said directly what the trial was *not* about. He said:

> It seems to me that I ought to first call your attention, because it will in my view follow, to the proof that no where in the charges and specifications thereunder which have been submitted to you and which form the foundation upon which this trial is to proceed, is there one word, one claim, one charge, even one suggestion that the accused, Staff Sergeant Matthew C. McKeon no matter what were the events of April 8, was either drunk, intoxicated, or under the influence of liquor in the slightest.[263]

He then said he thought it was important as the case went along "to know something of the accused." Looking directly at the judges and speaking just loud enough for the press to hear and low enough to convey the seriousness of the start of his case, Berman then asked:

> Who is Staff Sergeant Matthew C. McKeon who stands on two charges of a serious nature...he is accused of manslaughter by virtue of oppression and culpable negligence...so far as culpable negligence is concerned. As we understand the meaning it's a reckless and complete indifference to the consequences of one's conduct, and so far as oppression is concerned, I doubt if you will find anywhere, anywhere in any branch of maritime service, going back to that time where it was lifted bodily from the laws of the Royal

---

263 Ibid., 28.

British Navy, where there is such a term. But in its common usage, oppression is the tyrannical use of power for one's own advantage. Who then was Sergeant McKeon? Here is a man who up to this moment and including this moment had an honorable period of service. He is thirty years old. This is no errant child, a man of family. Back in 1942, at the age when he was not yet 18, I need not remind this court what the events of this country were in 1942—he enlisted in the Navy, serving aboard the *SS Essex* a carrier that was constantly in combat areas in South Pacific waters...his career aboard that ship was honorable and for three and one half years he was engaged as a combat Navy man aboard that carrier...in 1948...he enlisted in the Marine Corps and his first enlistment was for four years...a re-enlistment from 1952 to 1955. This re-enlistment brought him to Korea for combat where he was with Fox Company Second battalion of the first Marine Division. He was there in charge of a machine gun section and later took over his entire platoon.[264]

Berman promised that the jury would hear evidence of his selection for drill-sergeant school, of his graduating from that school of ninety who started with him. He ended up ranking fourteenth of fifty-five potential drill sergeants who made it to graduation. Berman then transitioned by concluding as follows:

Sergeant McKeon is in truth as the evidence will show you, a fine Marine who, as is so typical of so many, is dedicated to the U.S. Marine Corps and to the mission of that Corps. Well then let's talk a moment, as the proof will indicate it to the next problem that is involved in this case. Who was the platoon? This platoon was not actually in any way either on the bad side or the good side...in fact a group that the drill instructor within the period of ten weeks was

---

264 Ibid.

devoted to, indeed his duty, to turn into sharp well disciplined, reflex responding to command, interdependent marines and such was his purpose. Now in connection with the training of this platoon it became obvious to the accused as a drill instructor, as it did to others, that in terms of the Marine Corps training this platoon was not sharp—it was undisciplined, it had some of the characteristics of that technical term which is indigenous to Parris Island called a herd. It was not that these were bad boys in any sense of the word, it was simply they were not taking seriously the training and the output for their training that a beginner has to think that is a serious business and that the drill instructor is trying to make marines of them.[265]

Berman described why the training happened. Berman spoke of the lack of seriousness demonstrated by the two incidents of lounging on the lawn and of the taking of seconds and thirds of deserts in violation of Sergeant Huff's orders on April 8, which led Sergeant McKeon to come to the decision to lead a night exercise. Sergeant McKeon was not feeling well, his back was in pain from a herniated disc, and he leaned on a stick for support as he walked his platoon toward Ribbon Creek. Berman described the creek bed and asked:

Coming off that bank, what was the water? The evidence was that this was two hours after high tide, the ebb tide had been on two hours when Sergeant McKeon entered the water in front, along parallel with the bank, at a time when the water has generally been described as anywhere from knee to waist, thigh high, and went in this marsh with his men behind and by the way, this oppressed unit, as the events went up to this point, considered it a lark. It was joking and to use the vernacular expression, quite a bit of kidding around, and Sergeant McKeon seriously led his men. So much a

---

265 Ibid., 29.

Marine was he that even occasionally when the light of a faint moon would shed upon water, he would say to the men nearest him to them, "When you are in combat keep out of the light. When you ford streams, keep to the bank." And other things he himself had learned from hard combat. After some thirty yards he then led his platoon, making a left turn, these men followed up behind, and then left again...at no time was the water beyond his chest, possibly his arm pits...he had a right to assume that these men would follow him in his path as they had been directed to do by him, but by this time when the turn was being made there was no real formation now, men were in groups and one of these groups apparently wandered out, for reasons that unhappily can never be explained here and in so doing got into the channel of the creek itself. There was in the quiet of that night a sharp cry of help of one man. Then Platoon 71 was panicked. Panic is a very difficult thing to describe to people who have never observed it. Whether it be the panic that struck Platoon 71, under the circumstances I have just told, or whether it be the panic of civilians when fire strikes a theater, whether it be a night club on fire, panic does not lead itself to order or discipline. It is sheer stark mad, unreasoning terror and so men started to grab belts, to jump on each other. Sergeant McKeon hearing this cry for help and not too good a swimmer himself but adequate, swam out brought one man in, and shouted as did one section leader to form a chain from the bank out so men could be helped. By this time, jumping on one another good swimmers were pulled under, one I'm sorry to say was a victim of this tragedy. Sergeant McKeon himself, going out was pulled down three times by one man. I venture to say had that lasted one more minute we would not have occasion to try this case at all...what was this march for, what was its purpose and what was intended to be accomplished by it? This thing will go down as one of the tragic accidents which our civilized community finds more and more multiplied, and which we shall prove to you was Mr. President and officers of the Court, that the mission of this command was to produce marines and to produce them within a period of time given to the drill instructor which at that time was ten weeks, that the mission and the methods employed to accomplish it was indeed part and parcel, the very warp and hoof by which this Corps has its wonderful traditions and its well-deserved history. We shall prove to you in our view that Sergeant McKeon was a dedicated member of that Corps, trying to accomplish its purpose, not for self-benefit, not for sadistic pleasure, not for casual indifference to life but for the dedicated purpose of making marines of those entrusted to him. These methods require no apology either by the Corps or by Sergeant McKeon, but if there be others that thinks so, that apology should not have to be made by the sergeant who is on trial.[266]

It was General Pate who first placed the Marine Corps on trial with Sergeant McKeon when he reported to the US Congress that in a very real sense the Corps was on trial, too. But it was Berman who placed the "esprit de corps" at the defense table next to Matt as a codefendant. In defending the Corps, Berman defended both Matt and those who served as Marines. By defending Marines training methods, Berman found the witnesses he was looking for.

Thus the trial began in a hot auditorium on Parris Island with an opening that presented the entire defense case, which would be echoed in the evidence throughout the trial and in closing arguments. The prosecution started with Captain Weddell, the depot adjutant, responsible for the depot files and all papers.[267] The prosecution introduced the depot orders through Weddell, including the prohibition of alcohol in the barracks and the prohibition of any swimming due to polluted waters. The defense asked if the trial counsel had asked Captain Weddell to look for one single order

---

266 Ibid., 32.
267 Ibid., 34.

that put the Ribbon Creek area out of bounds. He could not find one, nor could the prosecution produce any such order during the trial, just in the same manner that Colonel McKean could give General Pate no such order when asked for one. In the middle of the questioning of Weddell, a note for an emergency phone call came into Berman. Berman asked to be excused to take a call, ostensibly from General Pate.

As testimony began in the auditorium, the calls in the BOQ continued to come in from supportive Marines. The sheer number of calls coupled with the vehement objections by the prosecutor to any line of questioning concerning the practice of night marches forced us to narrow down the potential witnesses we were taking to ensure relevancy and reduce the risk of not being able to use these witnesses. First we were taking witnesses who had marched in mud or swamps. Then we were only going to take witnesses who had marched in mud and swamps since 1940 on, and then it was narrowed further to marches that occurred between 1950 and 1955 and they had to be in water (mud was no longer sufficient). But many stood ready to testify to training practices not unlike the one of April 8, 1956. It was the same acknowledgment that McKean wrote about later concerning the majority show of hands raised when he asked his crew if they participated in night marches. This was not evidence the Marine Corps prosecutor wanted in the courtroom, and he fought like hell to keep it out.

Berman could not get the question of custom and usage out without this prosecution war. This played out over and over in the early days of testimony. For instance, in the first week of trial, Thursday, July 19, Berman asked Sergeant Huff on his cross-examination the following question:

Sergeant Huff, do you know of a practice on Parris Island in the training of recruits with respect to the training of discipline as to whether a practice existed of a training method for the training of discipline and the inculpating or boosting of morals in the unit, as well as for the training of interdependence amongst the men of that unit or platoon of marching men at night into the boon docks, marshes swamp water or creek water in the waters abutting or within Parris Island?[268]

The prosecution jumped up and objected:

> May it please the court, we object to the question one on the basis that it is a leading question and this is in the nature of direct examination which as exceeded the scope of previous examination of the prosecution; and, or secondly, that this is an attempt to inject a custom, practice or usage, whatever you call it, which was objected to yesterday and if the court is ready to hear our argument, we have a strong argument on that point.[269]

This objection was simply that the prosecutor had not questioned Sergeant Huff about a practice of night marches. Berman responded:

> The form of the question I have not led I have not suggested an answer; I have simply directed attention to the field in which the testimony is cast. As far as the ruling of the Law Officer on the admissibility of a common practice, it is true there hasn't been any such ruling. As far as making the witness my own witness on this point, I agree that for his inquiry I am making this witness my witness.[270]

A bulk of the trial work might be summed up in Berman's response: *I am making this witness, this adverse witness, my witness.* Berman did that with every witness on the stand at the trial. He elicited favorable testimony from every prosecution witness gently but persuasively. Berman seized upon cross-examination to retrieve from every prosecution witness information that was helpful to his theory of the case, and in so doing, he made them his witnesses.

---

268 Ibid., 161.
269 Ibid.
270 Ibid.

Nonetheless, the prosecution's continuing objection to evidence of the past practice of night marches in the swamps created a serious question for the defense of whether the evidence of night marches in the custom and practice in training procedures would ever make it to the trial record. A wall of silence started at the court of inquiry in the Marine Corps's refusal to grant immunity for Marines on Parris Island who might testify about past night marches. It continued through the court-martial with a similar edict that precluded Marines from engaging in discussions with the press in the form of a warning not to violate Uniform Code of Military Justice, Article 37 (i.e., not to attempt to influence the outcome of a court-martial).[271] It was evidenced in the hard-fought-for access to the questionnaires that the Corps sent out to Marines and former Marines regarding their experience on Parris Island. When reviewed, the defense learned it was a questionnaire that omitted the question of past night marches. It was also a questionnaire stamped "For Official Use Only," which effectively precluded its use by the defense.[272]

Cementing the silence were the constant objections by the prosecution to the testimony of custom and practice. The objections by the prosecution juxtaposed Berman's public call for help that reached retired Marines who continued to call and travel to Parris Island. One response from Daniel Marlowe of Miami, Florida, that was reported by Jim Bishop in his column read: "Was in Platoon 273, first recruit Battalion, in 1951…under Drill Instructor Staff Sergeant Robert A. Olsen. Forced marches in Ribbon Creek area at night was routine for all platoons. Will testify at own expense or give affidavit."[273] The evidence was mounting over the wall of silence.

On Friday, July 20, Berman started the proceeding with a request to end the day's work early on Friday so that he could attend to a matter requiring his personal attention some distance from Parris Island. This business was a meeting with General Pate.

---

271 See note 254 above.

272 Bishop, *Jim Bishop: Reporter*, 148.

273 Ibid.

As the trial continued that day with Sergeant Huff's cross-examination, the battle over the scope of testimony Berman could ask of prosecution witnesses during cross-examination continued. The law officer then made it clear that the defense would finally prevail on this point:

> Law Officer: I want to say at the very outset that I am inclined to rule, on my research thus far of the question prior to the hearing of argument that evidence of custom or common practice with respect to night marches instituted or initiated by drill including evidence of the condition and place where such marches took place, is admissible, in connection with the allegation in specification 1 of charge 3 of death by culpable negligence. It is my present inclination that evidence of custom or common practice with respect to night marches is not admissible with respect to any of the other charges and specifications.
>
> Would first like to have defense counsel state his position. I would then like to have trial counsel briefly state his position.[274]

After the law officer outlined his expectations for the flow of argument, Berman rose from his seat and started simply and briefly. Based upon what the law officer just said, Berman knew he was at least going to rule favorably to the defense on the issue of letting the evidence of custom or common practice with respect to night marches instituted or initiated by drill instructors. This evidence would include the condition and place where such marches took place in connection with the allegation in specification one of charge three, death by culpable negligence. So he needed to say very little, and he did just that. Berman said:

> Briefly stated Mr. Law Officer, our position is—of course we are in complete accord with your view expressed that this evidence is, of necessity admissible on the charge of culpable negligence, since

---

274 Trial Transcript, 162.

the evidence has to do with or is evidence of the reasonableness of the conduct of the accused in connection with whether it was negligent, either culpable or simple negligence, the test always being was it the act of a reasonable and prudent person, so evidence of practices performed here are at least some evidence of reasonableness of that conduct.[275]

The legal argument that followed between the prosecution and the defense went on for a long period of time and is reflected in ten pages in the trial transcript.[276] It ended as it began with the law officer determining that "it is admissible. I will grant the motion…I will rule that evidence of other similar practices under the same or similar…circumstances will be held to be admissible."[277] It was a hard-fought-for ruling and singularly important to the defense.

Thereafter, the testimony of Sergeant Huff continued where it left off, at the prosecution's objection to evidence of custom and practice of night marches. Berman was finally able to ask Sergeant Huff:

I am asking you whether as a result of having been on Parris Island for almost two years prior to April 8, 1956, and with your knowledge and acquaintanceship of a great many drill instructors and other non-commissioned personnel at Parris Island, did you know of a practice for the purpose of training discipline and boosting morale, of taking platoons on night marches into the boondocks, swamps, marshes and waters in the area of parries Island?
Law Officer: You may answer sergeant.
Huff: Yes sir.
Berman: And was it a practice?
Huff: As far as I know, yes, sir.[278]

---

275 Ibid.
276 Ibid., 162–73.
277 Ibid., 172.
278 Ibid., 175.

Sergeant Huff testified that he had also told the platoon that if they did not snap out of their hockey, or fooling around, he intended to march them down by the swamps. Berman ended his questioning of Sergeant Huff in the way he would end almost all his questioning of the witnesses who knew Sergeant McKeon. He asked what Sergeant McKeon's reputation was, and Sergeant Huff answered:

> Like I said before Sir, Sergeant McKeon, as far as I am concerned is an outstanding Drill Instructor. He done his work, done it well, and to me he never seemed to complain.[279]

In the first week of trial, the prosecution laid the foundation: death certificates, orders such as he could find about swimming and training, and search efforts. Outside the courtroom, the heavy humid air sizzled with the calls and activity that had followed Berman's plea on national television for witnesses. Outside the courtroom, attorneys on the defense team researched the canons of military law for the definition of oppression and prepared arguments for trial on those charges. Other attorneys reviewed the questionnaires, and I telephoned Lt. Gen. Chesty Puller in his home in Virginia.

I have always wondered why Berman asked me to call. Maybe it was an acknowledgment of our efforts in lining up witnesses from Massachusetts to Parris Island to testify about the custom and practice of night marches. As we did that, Berman had been working on the top brass of the Marine Corps. Maybe it was because Berman thought that Lieutenant General Puller would respond well to a veteran and former prisoner of war in World War II. I'll never know for sure, but all these years later, I still remember calling General Puller and his wife answering the phone in a high, soft voice telling me that he was in the backyard. His wife, called "Chesty," with a slow emphasis on the center vowels that put forth an endearing command to the commanding general to come to the phone.

---

279 Ibid., 177.

When General Puller answered, I introduced myself. I told him I was Matt's brother-in-law and part of the defense team. I then explained that I had been working these many weeks to locate witnesses familiar with the training practices at Parris Island and asked whether he would be willing to testify about those training practices. He answered, "Tell me where and when."

By Friday, July 20, 1956, the defense had lined up General Puller as a witness and were on their way to securing the cooperation of General Pate. In the courtroom, the testimony of the recruits of Platoon Seventy-One began with Private Thomas Grabowski.[280] Private Grawboski repeated slowly and confidently, like the Marine he had become, the story of the field day, of the novena that night, of the joking on the way to the creek, and of the panic that broke out. Private Grawboski testified at trial:

> We followed Sergeant McKeon and were walking along looking at the side and he told us to stay in the shadow because the enemy could see us. Actually he was trying to teach us about combat. Then we started to move out, and Sergeant McKeon was ahead of me, and that's when I dropped and I tried to swim back and I heard that panic...that's where the panic struck out amongst the boys. They started yelling and I started to swim back and that's when I found O'Shea. He was trying to grab on top of me and I was taking him, and someone said "I'll take him" so I was swimming back and the current was strong and we formed this chain gang. Some boys gave me their clothes and I lost them, their boots. We pulled most of them into low water and then someone called "Everybody out."[281]

Berman's cross-examination of Grawboski was gentle as he brought the witnesses through the facts, gentle as he asked about the drill sergeant:

---

280 Ibid., 196.
281 Ibid., 198.

Question: Did you get the impression from anything that was said including anything that Sergeant McKeon said that the object of this march was to go swimming?
Answer: No sir. We thought actually it would be a lark and if we did go out there it would probably just be up to our waist and teach us that he really meant business and he would have discipline.[282]

Did the platoon have good discipline? Grawboski said no. Berman asked about the path they took, the location of the incident, and he asked again what happened to O'Shea. Grawboski said, "I was trying to swim back, and he grabbed onto to me."

Question: What happened to you?
Answer: I tried to take O'Shea in and someone said "I'll take over."
Question: Were you pulled under?
Answer: Just about up to my neck.
Question: What type of Drill Instructor was Sergeant McKeon?
Answer: He was a good one sir.
Question: Was he a patient man?
Answer: Yes sir he had a lot of it.
Question: A lot of what?
Answer: Patience.
Question: Did he take an interest in you and the other members of the platoon with respect to your personal affairs?
Answer: Yes sir.
Question: Did he try to teach you various things?
Answer: Yes sir.
Question: And was he brusque or rough or gruff about the way in which he taught you or impatient in the way in which he was instructing you?
Answer: No sir.

---

282 Ibid., 201.

Question: Had you as a member of the platoon, noticed anything about the way in which Sergeant McKeon was walking.

Answer: Yes sir. He had a limp; he used a stick to walk along with.

Question: And he said to you and all of those with you, "Follow me"?

Answer: Yes sir.

Question: Were you able in that night to observe, after the panic struck, whether or not Sergeant McKeon was doing anything in the water?

Answer: Trying to help others.[283]

Berman established a pattern in the questions he asked Platoon Seventy-One. He questioned them about what they saw and their place in the march and in the water. He asked the purpose of the march, and they answered that the march's purpose was to teach them. He asked about the platoon, whether it was disciplined. They all answered that no, it was not. He asked what effect if any the press had had on them. Berman's final question to all the members of Platoon Seventy-One was what type of drill sergeant was Staff Sergeant McKeon. They answered in their own words, with their own impressions, and almost every man praised Sergeant McKeon and his patience.

Through his cross-examination, Berman made the Marines of Platoon Seventy-One his witnesses. He obtained the specific details of the incident in Ribbon Creek while gently teasing out the gray tragic truth of April 8, 1956. There was a methodical strategy in the series of questions to each member of the platoon. But their responses were unscripted glimpses of tragedy, retrospection, and regret.

---

283 Ibid., 209.

CHAPTER TEN

———

ON SATURDAY, JULY 21, 1956, Berman traveled to Virginia to speak to General Pate. General Pate kept Berman waiting outside on the front porch of the Norfolk home of a relative that he was visiting.[284] Berman waited. He was a patient man. If General Pate was trying to insult Berman by keeping him waiting, it did not work. Berman was not easily insulted, not even by high-ranking generals. When General Pate came out to the porch to meet Berman, he did not ask the lawyer from New York into the house. The two sat on the front porch.

General Pate came eye to eye with New York City's finest trial attorney, who had come on behalf of a noncommissioned officer from working-town Worcester and had enlisted before he had finished high school. General Pate had underestimated that public opinion would turn against his wholesale early condemnation of the accused drill sergeant. Nor had he expected such a fight from seasoned and experienced attorneys who typically came at a greater expense than a drill sergeant's salary could muster. Thus, General Pate changed course and agreed that day on the porch to testify for the defense.

How did Berman convince Pate, the commandant of the Marine Corps, to testify for the defense in a court-martial initiated by the Marine Corps? Of this conversation with General Pate, Berman later revealed: "I

---

284 Fleming, *U.S. Marine Corps in Crisis*, 82; McKean, *Ribbon Creek*, 344.

told the General that it was the only way to get himself and the Marine Corps out of this jam."[285]

My Sunday morning was spent reviewing mail. Some of my work in the trial involved the synchronization of the Corps and the defense interests. I was a middleman of sorts, calling witnesses, calling General Puller, and reaching out to retired members of the Marine Corps. I was the brother-in-law advising the family of the status and progress of the case, and a liaison of the defense efforts between civilian lawyers and the Corps lawyers Major DeBarr and Colonel Valentin. Berman told me that the week to come would bring fireworks, and he asked to watch Major DeBarr's and Colonel Valentin's reaction. Colonel Valentin and Major DeBarr are two fine officers, but I thought they were betwixt and between in this case in the sense that if the Corps were to suffer, it might have impacted them negatively.

Sunday afternoon brought the defense team a respite for a few hours on the golf course. Howard Lester, Major DeBarr, Colonel Valentin, and I got in nine holes of golf. I shot a forty-two, which was exceptional for me.

Sunday night in Massachusetts, Anne finalized the details of her travel with her brothers Ned and Francis to Parris Island for the final half of the trial. Our children were between states, relatives, and friends for most of that summer. My parents had Michael, and Marianne was with our friends the Ryans on City Island. Tommy stayed with Mrs. McKeon in Worcester, and Regina stayed with Anne's sister, Ellen. Anne arrived Tuesday with Ned and Francis. Her attendance coincided with the prosecution's case in chief.

The dissection of every detail of April 8, 1956, continued inside the Parris Island auditorium on Monday morning where it left off Friday, through the testimony of Platoon Seventy-One. Barber's testimony would be similar to that of Grawboski. The prosecution had ended Friday with these questions:

---

285 Fleming, *U.S. Marine Corps in Crisis*, 82.

Question: Now tell me Private Barber. You say you stopped in the water. Now continue with your story.

Answer: I stopped in the water and a little while afterwards I heard some fellows yelling for help but I couldn't do anything myself because I knew I couldn't swim so I yelled out to form a chain. There was about ten of us, we tried to form—had formed a chain but nothing become of it, so after a while in the water Sergeant McKeon ordered us out...

Question: All right now what happened after this excitement started?

Answer: It become quite of a panic, I believe, and people yelling and after we formed the chain to try to help the other fellows, but it didn't quite amount to anything, stayed in there a few minutes and then we got the word to go ashore, we went ashore and as we were going ashore a lot of us were slipping in the mud going back. We made it up the bank and went across a little ditch and up sort of like a hill and we stayed up there. Sergeant McKeon came back, we fell in a platoon formation to find out if anybody was missing. Sergeant McKeon said "I know we lost Wood."[286]

Cross-examination of Private Barber began on Monday. During cross-examination, Berman established the details of the swimming lessons Barber underwent. Thereafter, he probed the issue of discipline, which was a recurring theme with every witness he questioned.

Question: Now after your graduation as a recruit and now that you are a private in the Marine Corps, and thinking back on it on the basis of your own experience over those many weeks as a Marine, what would you say was the discipline of Platoon 71 at the time that this march and exercise was ordered?

---

286 Trial Transcript, 232.

Answer: In my opinion they didn't have too much discipline in the platoon...

Question: Well did you feel that the platoon, as such, not any one individual member, but that the platoon as a unit were sharp and serious in their work?

Answer: I wouldn't say they were very serious about it, but they took certain matters very seriously and others they didn't.[287]

Berman ended his questioning of Barber as he did all the witnesses of Platoon Seventy-One by asking:

Question: All right, in the five weeks that you had been in this platoon with sergeant McKeon as your Drill Instructor, tell us what kind of Drill instructor he was as far as you're concerned?

Answer: To me he seemed like a very right person. I mean he helped you if you needed any help, tried to help you.

Question: Was he patient or did he flare up?

Answer: No sir he didn't flare up he was a very patient person.

Question: Did he abuse anybody?

Answer: No sir. I didn't believe he did.[288]

The questions successfully negated the charge of oppression of the troops, and they chipped away at the prosecution theory of a heartless drill sergeant. In all, nineteen Marines of Platoon Seventy-One testified about the events of April 8, 1956, which I have outlined in previous chapters as best I could. Yet questions remain all these years later—or rather questions plague all these years later. Who first jumped on Wood as he pleaded for him to get off? Why didn't Thompson walk up to the grass? Was he in shock? How did the best swimmer of them, Hardeman...how did he die? How did he drown? Why didn't anybody see him? What happened

---

287 Ibid. 237.
288 Ibid. 244.

to O'Shea, Reilly, and Thomas? *What exactly happened?* It is a tragic but true fact that after the trial and after these more than fifty years, no one knows precisely those answers except to know that a deadly panic broke and nearly broke the spirit of the corps.

At the end of the recruits' testimony, Sergeant McKeon's statement that was given to the Corps investigator on the night of April 8 was entered. The investigator testified that it did not appear that Sergeant McKeon was trying to hide anything but had been completely cooperative and forthcoming.

On Tuesday, July 24, 1956, the court opened at 9:05 a.m. with a request from Berman for the prosecution to subpoena 108 former Marines. The law officer requested exact compliance with the rules governing court-martials, which included an offering of proof of the precise nature of the testimony. Berman could not use the questionnaires he finally had access to, but he could certainly subpoena the many former Marines who were familiar with the practices of Parris Island and of night marches. These Marines knew what Bishop referred to in his columns as "noncom country,"[289] where commissioned officers like General Burger on April 8, 1956, "played golf" and the work of turning boys into fearless Marines in a few weeks fell to noncommissioned officers.

Thursday, July 26, 1956, was the most crucial day of the trial thus far. Berman proved through the prosecution witness Dr. Atcheson that Matt McKeon was sober at 9:00 p.m. on April 8, 1956, less than one hour after the tragedy. Going forward the case would be decided on its merits concerning the action and decision of the march itself. Charges of oppression and intoxication were surely being dismantled in cross-examination, but Berman's work on Dr. Atcheson was a piece of art.

The direct examination of Dr. Atcheson was approximately four pages in the trial transcript. The cross-examination, a few pages of redirect and

---

289 Bishop, *Jim Bishop: Reporter*, 148.

more cross-examination, continued for twenty-four pages.[290] Berman started the cross by asking about the testing for sobriety. He continued:

Question: And do you know that it is testing, testings which have
to do with the coordination and activities of the central nervous
system, isn't that so, the brain and central nervous system?
Answer: Yes an objective test.
Question: And of course the matter of sobriety or lack of it is a
matter of the reaction of the brain to alcohol, isn't that so, generally
speaking?
Answer: Yes, generally speaking.
Question: So the way that that is tested medically is to test these
centers which emanate in the brain and which have to do with the
coordination of muscles and activities, isn't that right?
Answer: Yes.
Question: Now first of all you made such a test and that was per-
formed by you as a medical man, isn't that correct?
Answer: Yes sir.[291]

After a few more questions about the tests performed, Berman
continued:

Question: All right, tell us what were these tests?
Answer: One test is the test for equilibrium which I asked the ser-
geant to stand with his feet close together and shut his eyes and to
see how well he could stand up under the circumstances.
Question: Without swaying?
Answer: Yes.
Question: That has a name hasn't it, in neurological testing, called
the Rhomberg test?
Answer: Yes.

---

290   Trial Transcript, 503–27.
291   Ibid., 504.

Question: And that a perceptive test to find out about coordination and in your case you subjected him to that test or required him to perform that test?

Answer: Yes.

Question: Under your careful observation?

Answer: Yes.

Question: And was that test positive or negative?

Answer: The test was negative.

Question: And when you say the test was negative, his response to this neurological test for coordination meant it was within normal limits.

Answer: That is right.[292]

Similarly, Berman brought out the normal findings through the other tests that Dr. Atcheson performed, including the double-vision test; pulse rate, regularity and irregularity; observation of gait while walking; walking a straight line; observation of speech; testing pupils for reactions to light; pass pointing, meaning able to point without swaying; and coordination and reflexes. All these tests' results were normal. Finally, Dr. Atcheson was asked:

Question: Now I want to ask you Dr. Atcheson, on the basis of your tests, your observation, and the official request made of you to evaluate the sergeant's sobriety, do you have an opinion now with a reasonable degree of medical certainty as to whether or not the sergeant was within all the normal sobriety limits?

Answer: Yes sir he was within normal limits.

Question: Of sobriety?

Answer: Yes sir.[293]

---

292 Ibid., 504–5.
293 Ibid., 510.

As to the Bogen's test, Dr. Atcheson testified that he gave the Bogen's test no credence in light of his clinical findings and he could not say whether the syringe that the Bogen's test was performed with had been swabbed with alcohol because he was not the one who prepared that syringe. Berman next brought Atcheson through the details of the Bogen's test itself, which Berman knew Atcheson found unreliable since he had testified to as much in the inquiry proceedings.

After a series of questions regarding the Bogen's test and intoxication, Atcheson stated:

Answer: My opinion was that Sergeant McKeon was not clinically intoxicated, drunk or under the influence of alcohol. However in view of the fact that as carried out by the several test and questions involved on that form—in view of the fact that his breath was suggestive of alcohol to me and a point there which maybe I shouldn't bring out, which I think has a significant answer.
Question: What is that?
Answer: One with regard to what the patient has had to drink. That's of course, a question which I put to the Sergeant.
Question: What was it?
Answer: As I recall to the best of my recollection, he answered, "I had a few drinks or a few shots of vodka this afternoon." In view of the fact...in view of the finding that I had namely, odor of alcohol, suggestive odor of alcohol on the sergeant's breath, and the fact that he admitted having had something to drink, I concluded—which is a moot question—he may have possibly been under the influence of alcohol to a sub-clinical degree which no one, of course can determine. Clinically he was not intoxicated.[294]

---

294 Ibid., 521.

After a series of objections and colloquy among counsel, Berman asked again:

> Question: In other words your conclusion, then and now, in the best opinion you have with the reasonable degree of medical certainty is that this man was not intoxicated or under the influence of liquor or anything else on any basis that you could discover isn't that so?
> Answer: Sergeant McKeon was not clinically under the influence of alcohol as far as I could determine.[295]

The president of the court had the final word. Colonel Hutchinson asked Dr. Atcheson:

> Question: We should assume then Doctor, that in view of your answers to the questions that you have been asked that the question to number 7 here, which says "clinical evidence of intoxication" and the words "yes" and "no" follow and you circled "yes." You should have circled, "No." Is that correct?
> Answer: Yes, I would say no.[296]

The prosecution rested soon after. Berman reserved defense motions regarding the prosecution case until Monday. The week came to a close with a request from Berman to end early Thursday for a long weekend. Only one reporter knew where Berman was going. Jim Bishop reported that Berman's daughter wrote him a card and asked him if he could come to see her for her birthday. She would be eight, and Berman would be present at his home in Roslyn to celebrate.[297]

---

295 Ibid., 524.
296 Ibid., 449–26.
297 Bishop, *Jim Bishop: Reporter*, 149.

The effective cross-examination of Dr. Atcheson stole the prosecution's spotlight in closing its case in chief. The headlines on almost every newspaper of Friday, July 27, 1956 rang out: "Sergeant McKeon Was Sober." Jim Bishop said, "The family can say give him ten years, the curse was off."

CHAPTER ELEVEN

––––

ON SATURDAY MORNING I ROSE for a game of golf in warm morning breezes that momentarily dispelled work. On the course, I shot an eighty-nine. I had a real hot back nine, coming in with a forty. The respite of golf on Parris Island over the long weekend was not to last. Mort Janklow had returned to Parris Island. Berman was out of town. Almost all counsel had gone home over the weekend except me. It did not make sense to me to travel all that distance only to return on Sunday, so I stayed on Parris Island. I hate to think what might have happened if I had not stayed back.

Mort Janklow had traveled to Parris Island from New York City on Saturday, July 28, with one purpose only, and it was not, in my opinion, a purpose that served Matt's interests on trial in any way. Mort wanted to buy an option for the rights to tell Matt's story in the movies. Mort's offer? One thousand dollars. To me, it was one thousand dollars that would have sold the trial down the drain. I imagined then and now what the headlines on Monday morning entering the defense case would have read: "Sergeant Sells Story of Fatal Drowning to Hollywood for One Thousand Dollars." News like that could have overshadowed all our work. News of that nature might have made Marine Corps witnesses who were scheduled to testify potentially withdraw their support and walk away. Matt might have been convicted of the highest charges. Selling a story for profit in the middle of trial is all anyone would have remembered if Mort had succeeded in his sale. The only thing between Mort and Matt that weekend was my dislike for travel that kept me behind on Parris Island.

Mort's wife had an uncle in the movie business. Mort's promise of one thousand dollars was a lot of money back then. One thousand dollars was a fortune to a man with two children and a third on the way who was not sure if he was facing jail and a future of no income. Just as Matt's trial was turning for the better, Mort came in surrounded with the smell of a swamp breeze in his clothes and a poisonous promise on his breath.

Matt did not know what to say at first. He was considering it because of the financial uncertainty of his future. I did not think it was a good idea, and I told him so. Every time I think of it, I thank God that I was there on that island that weekend. I insisted that Matt talk to Berman before he even consider such a thing or make any decisions. Matt agreed to wait and talk to Berman before making a decision. Berman's response was, hell no. Matt said no to Mort Janklow, who thankfully left Parris Island empty-handed.

I remember that Matt was a physical wreck from the tragedy and trial, and he was so terribly broke. Mort knew he was broke because many years later Mort wrote that he didn't think "this guy" had any money. So Mort thought he might buy the movie rights.[298] That "guy," my brother-in-law, did not have any money, and he was not going to take Mort's promise of money in the middle of a trial for involuntary manslaughter.

By the time Berman returned to Parris Island on Sunday, July 29, he had a full lineup of witnesses for the defense. Berman believed that with General Pate and General Puller on board, he might be able to finish the case by Friday. We entered the week with an anticipation that we could knock out the most serious charges: charge two (oppression of troops) and charge three (involuntary manslaughter).

---

298 Larry Smith, *The Few and the Proud, Marine Corps Drill Instructors in Their Own Words*, Chapter Nine, Mort Janklow, Assisting Attorney, court-martial of Matthew C. McKeon, June–August 1956 (W.W. Norton & Company, New York), 126.

On Monday, July 30, the defense case started after all our motions to dismiss were denied. The first defense witness was Sergeant Scarborough. His testimony was brief and offered that the vodka was his, they both had a drink in the morning, he saw Platoon Seventy-One lying all around the grass, and Matt brought him to the noncommissioned officers club that afternoon on his way to get the mail. He also said the amount in the bottle marked in evidence was the same amount he recalled leaving there in the morning, which indicated that Matt had not drank any more vodka after Scarborough left it in his room that morning. The prosecutor on cross of Scarborough brought out that at the time of the court of inquiry, Scarborough testified he could not say how much was left in the bottle. But Berman had the last word, as he asked Scarborough on redirect:

> Question: Well I understand you to say here that you didn't know exactly how many inches or how much quantity was left in the bottle. Is that right?
> Answer: That's correct sir.
> Question: Did anybody show you the bottle when you testified at the board of inquiry, and asked you what was the amount left in it?
> Answer: No sir they didn't.
> Question: Did anyone ask you whether there was anything left in it at all?
> Answer: No sir they didn't.
> Question: In other words they just wanted to know if you could testify as to how much was left in it and you said you couldn't ?
> Answer: That is right sir.[299]

There were no other questions. Berman made his point. Without looking at the bottle, Scarborough could not say for sure how much was in it, but when shown the bottle, he could estimate that the amount was the same.

---

299 Trial Transcript, 606–7.

The next defense witness was United States Marine Corps Warrant Officer Leslie Volle, Second Topographic Company, Camp Lejeune, North Carolina. His military-occupation specialty was photo topographer, map compiler, 1440 MOS. Volle was a surveyor for five years, and in the past three years, he had specialized in hydrographic surveying. Volle's testimony established that the current or velocity of the creek was 1.2 miles an hour, or 1.05 knots per hour. At that velocity the creek would move at a distance of 1.7 feet per second. This is considered a slow-moving stream. A normal stream flow is three miles an hour.[300]

Volle also testified that Ribbon Creek at its mouth was obstructed with sandbars, which would have restricted the flow of water at high tide: "It would keep the water from reaching the maximum tide predicted for the area. In all probability the height predicted was never reached due to the obstruction at the mouth." As to the contour of the creek bed itself, Volle testified that the platoon would have had to have gone forty-eight feet toward the center of the creek from the point they entered the edge of the water of the creek to get to a depth of five feet. He was asked:

Question: So they would have to proceed from the time they hit water to 45 feet out directly to the center of the channel before they would be in water that was five foot deep?
Answer: That is correct.
Question: Is there any time along this line where they could take a step and step into the water that would go completely over their heads?
Answer: No sir.
Question: What is the gradient along that line?
Answer: Approximately one in ten. Just a little steeper than that.
Question: For every ten feet they would walk there would be a foot of water?
Answer: That is correct.

---

300 Ibid., 615.

Question: Now is that considered a very steep grading?
Answer: No sir, it isn't.
Question: Then a person walking directly out to the center of the stream through the channel would gradually go into the water?
Answer: That is correct.
Question: And at no time could he take one step or possibly two steps and go under water over his head?
Answer: No sir.[301]

Volle further testified that a person would have to go out twenty-eight feet toward the center before ever reaching five feet of water. Volle drew a line on a map representing a distance of approximately eighty-three feet and was asked:

Question: Now Mr. Volle if you pursued that second line is there any place that a man walking directly out into midstream towards the channel where he could take one step and go into water immediately over his head?
Answer: No sir, there isn't.
Question: But the man would have to go twenty eight feet out with the first contact with water before he would be in water five foot?
Answer: Yes sir.
Question: And at no time would he fall into a hole, cliff, Spanish well or any other kind of depression?
Answer: No sir. He would not. That is easy to determine because at low water at which time we were down there this bank from this zero point up beyond above which all of our measurements have proceeded so far is visible. Any holes would easily be seen by the naked eye. If you were in a boat out here or possibly on the pier looking back you could see it.

---

301 Ibid., 619–20.

Question: Well in fact Mr. Volle, there are no holes in the entire map area depicted?
Answer: That is correct. We could find no evidence of a hole.[302]

Berman reiterated the gradual gradient of the creek bed by asking:

Question: Just to re-emphasize again, Mr. Volle, in all your search over a period of ten days did you ever find any fall off, any cliff, any hole, any Spanish well or any depression whatsoever where a man could take one step or two steps and go into water immediately that was over his head?
Answer: No sir, we did not.
Question: And the bottom of Ribbon Creek, then, is a gradual gradient?
Answer: That is true; it varies but it will have to be considered a gradual gradient. There is no slope less than one to one; there is no place where we could find a one to one.
Question: Again for emphasis would you again repeat the speed of this current?
Answer: This current when the outgoing tide is similar, trying to duplicate the level on the night in question here, I got a velocity of one and two tenths per hour, which is not any great velocity whatsoever in the flow of the stream; its rather slow, in fact. Anything below three miles an hour is considered a slow stream.[303]

The prosecution pointed out that the measurements did not include any depth below mud that they may have sank into. There was a lot of banter between counsel about the prosecution's attempt to align the line-drawn map containing the route of the march to the photographic map used by the witness. The prosecution was able to bring out that from the drawings

---

302 Ibid., 621.
303 Ibid., 625.

of earlier exhibits. It appeared that the march went out for a distance of about one-third into the creek itself. The defense established that the grade of the slope into the creek was gradual without any steep drops. With that testimony, the talk of trout holes became anecdotal, and the testimony about drop-offs in the creek bed became unreliable.

The next witness to testify for the defense was Lieutenant Kraynick, United States Naval Reserve, an orthopedic surgeon. Matt had seen him because of lower back pain. This pain was caused by a herniated disc impinging on the nerve in the spine. The pain caused Matt to use a broom handle for a cane, visibly limp throughout the day of April 8, 1956, and in a few more years, it would hasten a medical retirement from the Marine Corps. At the conclusion of the doctor's testimony, the prosecution moved to strike it in its entirety.[304] The motion was denied.

On Tuesday, July 31, 1956, S. Sgt. Matthew McKeon was called as a witness by his lawyer. Berman walked him through his wartime experience. Berman asked about his experience with night marches in his own Marine Corps training. There were plenty of objections from the prosecutor over that, as throughout the proceedings. Berman asked again:

Question: During the course of your boot training here at Parris Island in 1948 was your platoon taken into the marshes and boondocks, swamps and marshes of Parris Island?
Answer: Yes sir they were.
Question: Once or more than once?
Answer: On several occasions sir.
Question: And were you taken in by any superior?
Answer: Yes sir.
Question: Who?
Answer: The Drill Instructor.[305]

---

304 Ibid., 649–63.
305 Ibid., 681–82.

The objections by the prosecutor go on for approximately a page and half in the transcript. He was fighting hard to keep evidence of these marches out. Berman continued:

> Question: My question to you—and I withdraw the question on the record and re-frame it—is that when you had been taken into water above your knees did you say?
> Answer: Slightly above my knees.
> Question: In the area behind the rifle range did you refer to the area where there was a water and marsh and swamps, that combination of things which is called on this island "boondocks"?
> Answer: Yes sir[306]

More objections followed. The prosecutor maintained that the defense counsel was leading. He was overruled, and Berman continued:

> Question: Following your graduation with your platoon—withdrawn—by the way did you happen to remember the name of the drill instructor who you said took you there on several occasions?
> Answer: He was killed in Korea sir.
> Question: Do you know his name?
> Answer: Arriva, sir.
> Question: Do you know how it is spelled?
> Answer: No sir I don't...Captain.[307]

Matt testified to his teaching in Quantico and his service of thirteen months in Korea where he led a section of fifteen to twenty guns defending an area. After going over Matt's complete service, Berman took to Platoon Seventy-One. He testified that in the very beginning, they were outstanding.

---

306 Ibid., 684.
307 Ibid., 685.

Question: Tell us about this platoon as you observed it from that point on until this tragic April 8?

Answer: Well when we first picked this platoon up we immediately put them in shock and fear stage. This is usually not any violence or anything, but we keep them moving all the time. Up until about a week before we went to the range, maybe a few days before we went to the range, you could see the platoon kind of slacking off. They had spirit, they had good morale in it but I noticed the platoon was more or less working in groups. I suppose you could call it a buddy-buddy system. They weren't working as a unit and they were told about it. Then we went to the range. The big thing I could see was that the drill instructors weren't with them all the time.[308]

Matt testified that the eagerness to learn had left them and they moved slowly when called out to attention. He would correct them. And it seemed to work for a day or two, and then they seemed to slack off again.[309] Matt said:

Well I liked to have an honor platoon like any other drill instructor would, I suppose, but I always thought if they went off this island knowing something about discipline then they would go off the island with something...I always believed without discipline you have no foundation regardless. What you may put on top of that foundation in later years, the kid may become the best technician the Marine Corps has ever laid eyes on but when the chips were down if they didn't have that discipline the thing would crumble.[310]

The first hour of Matt's testimony concerned his extensive past service, his assessment of the platoon, and his motivation that day in April. After

---

308 Ibid., 691–92.
309 Ibid., 693.
310 Ibid., 694.

a brief recess, we returned to a packed auditorium in the consistent ninety-five-degree heat we were working in. In that sweltering summer heat in an overcrowded room, Matt took the stand again. The stillness in the air was pierced by his voice, steadily recounting the events of those days under the gentle questioning of his advocate. One could hear a background rush of air moved by the fans of the female spectators, pens scribbling notes by the many newsmen in the room, and Berman's high-pitched New York-accented voice subdued by the questions he asked. The answers were given by Matt with the steady sounds of a working-class New England accent. Matt wore his uniform. His body was tall and straight as he walked to the stand, fully clothed in his Marine Corps khakis. His pants seemed unable to find his thinness below and hung as though on a hanger with nothing in them.

There was nothing left to the man but his story to tell. He had been incarcerated for over three months, had stood before his family as a prisoner between two armed guards, had been examined mentally and physically by the Corps, had been written about in every newspaper in America, had been spoken about by almost every American, had been cursed and prayed for, had been both condemned and exonerated, and had been loved and hated. He had endured this all these many months until this day when his lawyer gave him this fighting chance as he sat on the hard witness chair before the seven men who held his fate, before the Marine Corps and the navy, before the press that began to give him the fairest shake of all, and before his family, I among them, who would never abandon him in his life or after.

Matt told them of the Sunday in spring that started in devotion and ended in death. The details were well known, and with each telling by each witness, the night seemed almost clear, then not. As they marched, some of the men drifted, preferring to wade than walk. Matt testified:

Answer: The reason I asked where the non-swimmers were was for the simple reason I didn't want those people wandering out or getting in any trouble. I didn't know that there were swimmers around them, but I supposed there were swimmers around them.

Question: At any rate you found they were in ranks with people around them?

Answer: Yes sir, they were in more or less columns of two's. They wouldn't have been covered down in column of two's in water; they were maybe six inches out of line; they wasn't covered down, if you know what I mean.

Question: You mean they were not in exactly a straight line; is that what you mean?

Answer: They wasn't behind the other.

Question: All right.

Answer: We started coming down and kept on coming down. A few of the men, I don't know who said it, but they wanted to swim across. I told them this is no swimming lesson. I said they would ignore going across.

Question: Go ahead.

Answer: At this time there was a group behind me—there was a moon on the water, I looked out and there was light on the water. I remember there was a moon, but there was real clouds, big, black clouds up there and rolling, and every now and then the moon went behind those clouds. I told the men if ever you are running a problem or ever in combat regarding crossing a body of water, always keep out of the light, keep close to the shore line, into the shadows. We were still coming down and I asked, again I asked where the non-swimmers were and if everybody was all right. At the time I asked where Private Leake was.

Question: What did you ask for him for?

Answer: Well old Leake he was my problem boy.

Question: Talk up. We can't hear you—he was what?

Answer: He was more or less my problem boy; he just couldn't do anything right at times. He really tried, he was a good kid and try-ing all the time and I think he will make a terrific Marine but at times he didn't do anything right.

Question: So you asked where is old Leake?

Answer: I asked where Leake was and back in the platoon some-one said, "Here's Leake," and I said bring him up here. At the time the platoon was going down like this [indicating] and the end of the platoon was going around making a circle. Leake... the rear end of that platoon I seen them coming across this way with Leake.

Question: Who was coming across with Leake?

Answer: There was two kids with their arms under his arms, two men had him. I left the front of the column and I went back.

Question: Did you hold up the column?

Answer: Yes sir the column held up there.

Question: In other words you went back partially to meet where Leake was being brought to you?

Answer: Yes sir.

Question: Go ahead.

Answer: At that time I recall the water and I recall the water for the simple reason I met Leake with these two guys standing next to him in water up to their hips, just over their hips, about to their waists. I asked Leake if he was scared. I told him he needn't be scared—I knew he was petrified, he was scared—and Leake said he was scared and I told the two guys that had him to take Leake in the back and watch Leake. I left Leake.

Question: Do you remember yes or no, do you remember whether you picked anything up out of the water and said anything in that connection?

Answer: Yes sir I do.

Question: All right what was that?

Answer: At the time that Leake came up I told Leake there was noth-ing to be scared about. Before I asked him if he was scared I broke off that grass, swamp grass, I call it, I don't know what you call it.

Question: Well that's all right, we call it marsh grass.

Answer: There was marsh grass about up to my thigh and it was rubbing alongside of my leg—

Question: In the water?

Answer: Yes sir.

Question: Go ahead.

Answer: I reached down and broke off a piece of it and said: These aren't snakes, Leake; this is only grass, Leake. I guess he didn't believe me. He didn't say anything. I could see his eyes. He was scared. I told them to take Leake back, take care of Leake, watch Leake. I went back and took up my position in front of the platoon. At that time we took maybe five feet and the water tapered off, the water was about up to there [indicating], never got any deeper or any lower, as I recall, about the second button, up there at the chest some place.

Question: Go ahead.

Answer: When I got back about the opposite the place we come in I figured it was about opposite the place we come in. I didn't have any marker to measure it—I was heading for that ditch—I could see the slope of the ditch and the bank always visible. I would say we were out no more than twenty five feet, possibly thirty—give it the benefit of the doubt and say thirty that a rough estimate.

Question: What were you heading for the ditch for?

Answer: It's there where I was figuring on coming out going up this ditch and going back in there behind Charlie Range.

Question: In other words, that is what you were going to take them through and out, is that correct?

Answer: Yes sir.

Question: You say at this point, the point you were going to tell us about, you figured you were just about at the place you went off the bank and into the water; is that correct—I mean opposite or on a line with it.

Answer: Yes sir.

Question: Where did you say that was?

Answer: Right about here in this position here, right about here [indicating on the exhibit]...

Question: Had you gotten back in front of that column?

Answer: Yes sir I was.

Question: Had you taken some additional steps?

Answer: Yes sir I took approximately five maybe six steps.

Question: Then what happened?

Answer: I just can't say what happened but something did happen.

Question: Well try to explain the best you can what it was.

Answer: Well, they started to yell, there was yelling; a big mad commotion is all I can say it was. I couldn't actually distinguish one word from the other to be frank with you.

Question: Where with respect to where you were did this noise and commotion come from?

Answer: It was in rear off to my right...

Question: What did you see? You haven't told us what you saw?

Answer: I turned around when all this yelling started—I didn't know what happened and I seen this group out there splashing in the water. I couldn't actually determine if the men were calling for help or what, but I seen them thrashing in the water and it looked like they were reaching for something. The next command I gave I said everyone out of the water I told them to get out of the water and I started swimming out toward this area here.

Question: You say you were standing in water which was no more than chest high. Why did you swim?

Answer: I knew it was the quickest way out; it was kind of tough walking there.

Question: Go ahead.

Answer: I started swimming out toward this area here where they were and there was a kid looked like he was going the wrong way; he had his back toward me. I latched onto his dungaree jacket and pulled him approximately oh maybe ten feet in toward the ditch, and I stood up and asked him if he could stand up and he said he was all right. He said he was all right and I left him there and I started back out toward this group which at the time was almost parallel with me...in other words instead of back there it was back here [indicating]. I started out and I seen this boy coming in, I seen this boy coming in. I thought he was going out all right and I was ignoring him for the simple reason that out there maybe five yards further there was a kid I could see the top of his head and I thought he was floating, That's the kid I was going for, but around this kid was possibly three or four splashing—wasn't screaming or yelling or nothing but they was splashing. I headed out toward that kid and as I went by this other boy, this other man, he latched onto me... well I can't just say—it surprised me—and when I did realize what happened the man had hold of my neck. I tried to break his hold and every time I started treading water the both of us went down. And as we come up I told the guy to keep his head and I'd get him in. He was a black boy. I don't know who it was but I think it was private Wood because I'd get hold of him and try to bring him around in front of me and he wouldn't leave go, and I was looking at him more or less like this and he wasn't saying anything, wasn't saying a thing. He went down second time and the second time he went down it seemed to me like he went down further than the first time. While down there all I was thinking of was getting to the top. I was pulling toward the top and this kid let go, this kid let go and that's the last I seen of him.[311]

Tears filled Matt's eyes, and Law Officer Klein said maybe this was a good time for a recess. I, too, had tears in my eyes. But Berman told Matt, "Buck up, soldier." He had to get his client through the rest of the direct examination. There were more details to go through: the

---

311 [311 Ibid.], 728–32.

count of the men, the statements, the MPs, and the arrest and then cross-examination.

Berman took Matt through the remainder of the testimony, and the cross-examination was set to start the next morning. At Berman's request, they started at 8:30 a.m. on Wednesday, August 1, because he had been advised that "a witness will be present tomorrow the necessities of whose office require that he take the stand no later than 1:15..." The witness was General Pate.

On Wednesday morning, Matt took the stand at 8:40 a.m. Cross-examination lasted two hours. In it, the prosecution effectively proved an element of negligence. The prosecutor asked:

Question: Now, had you ever entered Ribbon Creek at this place before?
Answer: No sir I never had.
Question: Had you ever been in Ribbon Creek before?
Answer: No sir I have never been...
Question: But you had never been in Ribbon Creek before?
Answer: No sir, I never was actually in the creek sir, no sir, I wasn't.
Question: Then you never made any type of reconnaissance that night?
Answer: No sir I didn't make any reconnaissance that night. Before I stepped off that bank I looked at it, it didn't look dangerous to me.[312]

Two hours of aggressive cross-examination ended with the prosecutor asking a series of questions pressing Matt on his previous written statements, which Matt did not recall.

Question: You don't recall that now?
Answer: No sir as I said before, Major, I don't recall what I said in that statement. Sergeant Cummins come in there stating that the General wanted a statement right away. I spoke into that tape

---

312 Ibid., 768–69.

recording machine first and then he shoved off with the tape recorder, I suppose. Major Holben come in and said, "Do you realize what you've done?" He sit down and started reading me out of a book. I didn't know what was going on.

Question: But you signed all that?

Answer: I would have signed anything sir, I would have walked to the gallows.[313]

By the close of Matt's testimony, he had admitted responsibility for drinking in barracks and admitted to negligence in failing to conduct reconnaissance prior to the march that night.

---

313 Ibid., 781.

CHAPTER TWELVE

———

ON THE AFTERNOON OF AUGUST 1, 1956, Gen. Randolph McCall Pate, commandant of the United States Marine Corps from 1956 to 1959, entered the building on Parris Island where the trial was being held. General Pate had been summoned by the New York defense counsel for the accused Marine Corps drill staff sergeant. General Pate was in full uniform and wore sunglasses that he did not remove throughout the proceedings.

Before taking the stand to testify, General Pate walked into defense counsel's room and was introduced to Sergeant McKeon. He extended his hand to Matt and said, "Sergeant, I am glad to meet you, but not under these circumstances. I came down here to help you. Is your wife here? I would like to meet her." Before he left the room, in a gesture of goodwill, he slapped Matt on the breast and said, "Good luck, Sergeant."

On the witness stand, General Pate went down the line for Matt as much as he could. He acquiesced that supervision of the drill sergeants by officers had "been slipping a little bit."[314] He offered that the drill sergeants had broad discretion to instill discipline, which is among the primary goals of training.[315] Berman asked General Pate whether a drill sergeant in an attempt to teach discipline, instill spirit, and develop an esprit de corps via an unscheduled march, if on a Sunday less than a thousand yards from the rifle range that drill sergeant marched his platoon into a swamp in

314 Ibid., 791.
315 Ibid., 793.

the creek, would General Pate call that oppression of troops? General Pate answered, "I wouldn't call that oppression, no."[316]

As Berman proceeded to ask a simple question of what General Pate thought should be the result of this case, the prosecutor objected vehemently that it was infringement on the court's determination. This forced Berman to pose his question in the formality of seeking an expert opinion. This did not work to the benefit of the prosecution in two important ways. Berman's question came into evidence, but rather than three lines, it took up two full pages in the trial transcript, allowing Berman to argue the facts favorably for a lengthy period of time in the form of seeking an expert opinion. Secondly, formality forced Berman to qualify General Pate as an expert, who then rendered an opinion less than helpful to the prosecution case. He answered:

In my opinion I probably...of course, there's no final say as to what an individual would do under all circumstances, and, of course, I have not had the evidence that has been introduced in this court. I think you have to take that into consideration. It is evident this platoon, this drill sergeant did drink some vodka and I assume that it was against the regulations, the conditions under which he did it. I don't know. I think maybe I would take a stripe away from him for such a thing like that. It's a fairly serious thing, of course, particularly when you are dealing with recruits.

As to the remaining part of it, that's a little fuzzy and hazy to as just what transpired but I suspect I would probably have transferred him away for stupidity, or, if you want to be more polite, for lack of judgement. I would probably have written in his service record book that under no conditions would this sergeant ever drill recruits again. I think I would let it go at that. That's not a final answer, I know—that's about what my judgement would be.[317]

---

316 Ibid.
317 Ibid., 801.

Berman made good on his promise to Colonel Valentin and Major DeBarr that it was not his intention to tear down the Corps but to defend the esprit de corps. And so he did with Marine Corps witnesses who ranged in rank from drill sergeants to commandants. But not the full eighteen he had requested subpoenas for, or the many who came to Parris Island in support of Matt and who were willing to testify about training practices. One of these witnesses, Sgt. Leland Blanding, testified truthfully and boldly that he was not only aware of the practice of unscheduled marches but he engaged in that training as a drill sergeant on Parris Island. The testimony of night marches came out in spite of rigorous objection by the prosecution. The prosecutor included in his objections requests to the court to admonish and warn Sergeant Blanding. Berman objected to the warning and argued that nothing Sergeant Blanding had said indicated a need for the warning. The prosecutor asked again for the court to warn Sergeant Blanding, but Sergeant Blanding remained unrepentant in his testimony and unafraid. The prosecution said, "I ask the Law Officer to warn this witness under Article 31 of the Uniform Code." The witness looked directly at the prosecution and said, "I understand the article fully, sir." The law officer asked:

Question: You understand?
Answer: I do.
Question: You don't require a warning?
Answer: No, sir, I don't, I know it fully.[318]

Sgt. Leland Blanding did not flinch. His testimony confirmed that night marches were part of the culture of training on Parris Island, in spite of threats and objections by the prosecution.

Next, James C. Flaherty, a retired Marine Corps drill sergeant, testified that during his fifteen months as a drill sergeant, he was aware of the practice of taking recruits into the swamps, waters, and marshes abounding Parris Island for the purpose of teaching discipline. The prosecution

---

318 Ibid., 820.

objected and put Sergeant Flaherty through a cross-examination that implied in one question that he disobeyed orders by going into the water with his recruits. Berman objected that there was never such an order until "last Thursday." The law officer ruled in favor of Berman and sustained his objection. He ruled again in his favor when Berman successfully objected to the question by the prosecutor: "While you were on active duty with the Marines, did you violate any order?" In other words, had Flaherty ever violated the Uniform Code of Military Justice? But the law officer would not allow it. Sergeant Flaherty left the stand and left intact the now-known practice of swamp marches.

The US Marines still bid Chesty Puller good night and add "wherever you are" in an invocation to his fighting, faithful spirit. On the afternoon of August 2, 1956, Lt. Gen. Lewis Puller, United States Marine Corps, retired, was on Parris Island to testify for the defendants, including the Marine Corps as included by General Pate in his speech to Congress that both the Marine Corps and Sergeant McKeon were on trial. Lt. Gen. Lewis Puller is the most legendary and highly decorated Marine in the history of the United States Marine Corps, then and now. He commanded the courtroom that day in every way.

Lt. Gen. Lewis Puller entered to a standing room. When he sat down at the witness chair, he pushed the microphone aside and said, "Can everyone hear me in the back?" A member of the defense team recalled that the heels of the Marines standing clicked loudly at attention and the sound reverberated like a gunshot as they responded with a salute and "Aye, aye, sir." In a voice that everyone could hear, he testified about his background and what he learned in training on Parris Island as a young recruit:

Well, the main I learned here as a recruit that I have remembered all my life, is that I was taught the definition of the esprit de corps. Now my definition, the definition I was taught, that I've always believed in, is that esprit de corps means love for one's own military legion; in my case the United States Marine Corps. It means more than self-preservation, religion, or patriotism. I also learned that this loyalty to one's corps travel both ways, up and down.[319]

Before Berman asked Lt. Gen. Lewis Puller to go over his training, he asked permission to sit down. Berman was not tired, but he was doing the best thing a trial lawyer can do on direct testimony of his or her witness: become as invisible as possible.

Lt. Gen. Lewis Puller testified that he was trained at Parris Island, attended noncommissioned officers school on the island, and trained recruits on Parris Island and in San Diego. After World War I, he served overseas and had been commissioned a second lieutenant. Thereafter, the budget for the United States Marine Corps was drastically cut, and he lost his commission but reenlisted in the Marines and was assigned as an instructor and an officer in the Gendarmes de 880. After five years, he was again commissioned as an officer and returned to the States for a year of duty as an artilleryman. He was ordered then to Marine barracks at Pearl Harbor, where he stayed for two years. In May of 1928, he was ordered to Nicaragua as an instructor and officer, where he stayed until January 1933. He was legation guard to the American Embassy Guard in Peking until 1934, when he was ordered to command the Marine detachment aboard the USS *Augusta*, a flagship of the Asiatic station. In 1939, he returned to China for duty in the Fourth Regiment Shanghai. In 1941 he became the commanding officer of the First Battalion, Seventh Regiment of the First Marine Division. He remained stationed in Camp Lejeune until the Seventh Regiment was formed into a brigade and went to British Samoa. He testified:

"I remained in British Samoa with the Brigade until the landing at Guadalcanal. I led the First Battalion of the Seventh through the fighting on Guadalcanal and then the First Division was pulled out."[320]

---

319 Ibid., 840.
320 Ibid., 841.

After a period they went to the Russell Islands to get ready for the Peleliu operation. After the Peleliu operation, he returned to the States and was assigned as with the First Training Regiment at Camp Lejeune. After a year at Camp Lejeune, he served in New Orleans from 1946 to 1949. He commanded the Marine barracks in Pearl Harbor from 1948 to 1950. In 1950, he was ordered to Camp Pendleton to command the First Regiment of the First Division again. The First Regiment went to Korea and served in combat for seven months. He was returned to the United States and assigned to duty as a brigade commander at Camp Pendleton, California. He detached again and returned to Camp Lejeune to command the Second Division.[321]

Lt. Gen. Lewis Puller's recitation of his background did not include the descriptions of his battles, of actions that saved his company by hailing a coast-guard carrier in Guadalcanal, of holding Henderson Air Field in Guadalcanal, or of blood-soaked battles of brave Marines in Peleliu. It was an understated and humble recitation. As to his decorations, Berman asked, without going into all the decorations: "I have read somewhere… is it true that you have been decorated with five Navy Crosses?" Chesty answered simply, "Yes."

In response to Berman's questions, Lt. Gen. Lewis Puller defined the mission of the United States Marine Corps from the:

…time that General Von Stueben wrote the regulations for General George Washington, the definition of the object of military training is success in battle. In my opinion that is the only object of military training. It wouldn't be any sense to have a military organization on the backs of the American taxpayers with any other definition. I've believed that ever since I have been a Marine.[322]

Berman asked what was the most important training a recruit can receive. Lt. Gen. Lewis Puller responded:

321 Ibid., 840–1.
322 Ibid., 842.

Well, I'll quote Napoleon. Napoleon stated that the most important thing in military training was discipline. Without discipline an army became a mob.[323]

As with General Pate, Berman asked Lt. Gen. Lewis Puller his expert opinion. Berman said:

> I want you to assume what is the evidence in this case, that a drill instructor on a Sunday evening in an effort and in an attempt to teach discipline and instill morale into a platoon which he considered had poor discipline and no spirit, that he turned them out and marched them by leading them across the Rifle Range and leading them at the head of the column into the marshes and water at their head without regard to the results. Do you have an opinion which you can state with a reasonable degree of certainty as to whether or not from the point of view of a military man such as yourself this is an oppression of troops?[324]

Lt. Gen. Lewis Puller answered, "In my opinion, it is not." Berman then queried.

> Question: Well now based again on your long and extensive positions of command that you have held throughout your life can you state within a reasonable degree of certainty as to whether the leading the troops by the one who commands then is or is not a good practice?

Lt. Gen. Lewis Puller responded, "Any kind of commander or leader is not worth his salt who does not lead his troops under all conditions."[325]

---

323 Ibid.
324 Ibid., 844.
325 Ibid., 845.

Question: I take it then that your answer is that it is a good practice?
Answer: Yes, it is an excellent practice.[326]

Berman continued with the very long hypothetical that included all the facts of the case and asked whether leading the men into the swamps for the purpose of discipline was a good or bad military practice. Lt. Gen. Lewis Puller answered:

Answer: In my opinion the reason that American troops made out so poorly in the Korean War was mostly due to lack of night training. If we are going to win the next war I would say that from now on fifty percent of the training time should be allotted to night training.
Question: So in your opinion was this act of this drill instructor in leading his troops under those conditions and for that purpose, good or bad military practice?
Answer: Good.[327]

On cross-examination Lt. Gen. Lewis Puller confirmed thus: "You are supposed to make a reconnaissance when you are in battle." But there were no other critical points the prosecution could get from Lt. Gen. Lewis Puller. The prosecutor asked:

Question: No one will dispute the necessity for training. However do you believe that night training should be the initial training that a raw recruit should receive?
Answer: Well the trouble is that not enough night training is prescribed.
Question: Yes but…

326 Ibid.
327 Ibid., 846–7.

There were no "ands, ifs, or buts" for Chesty when he answered:

> And I know that in anything I have ever commanded I got most
> of the glory and I got all of the blame. I have willingly taken the
> blame I would train my troops as I thought—as I knew they should
> be trained regardless of a directive.[328]

Here, the prosecutor broke a cardinal rule of cross-examinations, which is
not to ask questions you do not know the answer to. The prosecutor asked
more questions, and none proved helpful to his case. He asked a hypothetical about taking nonswimmers out without safety precautions to which
Chesty answered:

> Answer: I would say this night march was and is a deplorable accident.
> Question: Would you take any action against me if I were the one
> who did that, if you were my commanding officer, Sir?
> Answer: Since I have been retired there was an accident similar to
> this down on the Florida Keys. It concerned the American Army.
> A soldier acting coxswain of a landing craft, took his landing craft
> around and outside the breakwater. The landing craft filled and
> sank. Seventeen soldiers were drowned. It hardly made the news-
> papers. As far as I know, there was no general court martial—or
> any kind of disciplinary action. I think from what I read in the
> newspapers yesterday of the testimony of General Randolph Pate
> before this court, that he agrees and regrets that this man was ever
> tried by general court martial.[329]

Lt. Gen. Lewis Puller dominated the tension-filled courtroom for the dramatic hour that he testified. His testimony was so strong that Berman
rested immediately thereafter. Thirty-three defense witnesses in the wings

---

328 Ibid., 848.
329 Ibid., 850.

under subpoena would not be necessary. Berman had put on sufficient evidence with the testimony of General Pate, the commander of the Marine Corps, and of Lt. Gen. Lewis Puller, the Marine Corps commander of esprit de corps.

The entire audience in the courtroom stood as Lt. Gen. Lewis Puller walked from the room. Those in the service stood at attention and saluted as he passed, and Jim Bishop observed and wrote in his column that "a few were misty eyed."[330] Matt's back slumped forward for the first time in this long trial, and the wait for a verdict would soon begin after closing arguments.

At the NCO club that night, when Chesty entered the club, a roar of applause sounded for him from everyone in the club. Chesty came over to Anne and asked her with great confidence and a generous heart: "When are they going to release Matt?"

On the day the verdict came in, Matt and Berman stood and faced the judges. He was found not guilty of the most serious charges of oppression of the troops and reckless homicide but found guilty of drinking in barracks and negligence for his failure to perform reconnaissance. The lawyer from New York City, standing shoulder to shoulder with Matt, faced the reading of the verdict. Berman began weeping even as he stood still at attention before the judges. Anne was weeping, and I could see that there was no more coffee in her future. Her bargain with God came due.

The next day, the judges hit Matt pretty hard on sentencing: nine months hard labor and a bad conduct discharge. The hard working record on appeal that Berman built proved invaluable, because the sentence was later reduced by the secretary of the navy to three months and demotion to private. Matt had already served six and a half weeks in the brig and had been confined for several months thereafter. In reducing the sentence and allowing Matt to remain in the Corps, the secretary of the navy noted that nowhere but in the military service is negligence a criminal offense. Matt was later promoted to corporal and retired on medical disability. Freedom was his then and remains his now.

---

330 Bishop, *Jim Bishop: Reporter*, 159.

Conclusion

————

ON THE NIGHT OF SEPTEMBER 21, 2004, my mother, Anne McKeon Costello, began spitting up blood as a result of advanced stomach cancer. I was with her on City Island because I had that day attended the funeral of my best friend's mother, Barbara. After saying my final good-bye to Barbara, I spent that night catching my mother's blood in her pink bath towels. When her stomach quieted momentarily, she looked out her bedroom window onto the darkened night water of the bay as though reaching for answers and for more time. The dark water of the bay that was so familiar to her after fifty years on City Island answered her with the silence of secrets kept.

That night, my mother had to decide to go into either the hospital or hospice. When I asked her where I should take her, she waved her hand with three fingers together and her ring and pinky finger bent into her palm in a gesture I saw my whole life that communicated the firm resolution of how things are, like it or not. She said, "Well, I am terminal, so I'll go to hospice." She was not crying or scared. In the morning, we rode to Calvary Hospice in an ambulance, my mother strapped to a gurney and I and my father strapped to a seat.

Calvary had been the first hospice of its kind in a nation where cancer is now an epidemic, and though a hospice, it was and remains a hospice of healing. After my mother was admitted to Calvary, the attendants rolled her gurney into an elevator. The elevator doors opened to an image of Saint

Therese on the wall of the floor. This floor of Calvary my mother spent her last days on was dedicated to Saint Therese, my mother's patron saint. After all these many years of prayers to Saint Therese for intercession, especially in 1956, Therese did not answer with silence but answered with a sign, just as she had done in 1956 with roses in the hospital for my grandmother, Alice McKeon. A priest in Calvary administered the last rites as my mother slept under the prayerful eyes of her patron, Saint Therese. I remember prayers the most from that first day I spent with my mother in Calvary, and I cannot forget my mother's voice saying, "In difficult times, Marie Therese, just pray, just pray." Prayer was always her answer.

In her final days, Saint Therese and the sweet nuns from City Island convent watched over my mother, a nun from Ireland kneeling by her bedside as she slept said in a thick Irish brogue, "She is going straight up, straight up." The nuns, wearing the heavy gray garments of their devotion, with white-banded gray veils on their heads, knelt at her bedside in prayer. They did not pray for her soul to pass to heaven, because they believed she was on her way. They prayed for her suffering to be minimal. It was not. She could not eat, could not drink, and was heavily medicated at times because of the pain. An IV in her wrist administered medication and liquids. Swallowing made her so sick, but she tried for our sake until the doctor said, "Anne, tell them you can't." I stopped offering ice cubes. The words "I cannot" had never before been in her vocabulary. Her body was failing but her steadfast faith and hope remained constant. In Calvary, she told her five children, myself included: "I have taught to you how to live, and now I am going to teach you how to die," which she did with a quiet dignity.

How had she lived? She remained committed to my father even though he drank. I remember the sounds of his drinking either in the sad tunes of the Irish tenor John McCormack he played through the night into the early hours of morning or in the sound of him yelling in German, haunted by the days of his imprisonment in a German prison camp in World War II. She stayed with him through it all, good and bad, better or worse, in sickness and in health, and held him up at all times. He said she tricked him into quitting the booze by sending him to her doctor for a stubborn cut he had on his leg that would not heal. He returned from her doctor knowing his health was failing, potentially fatally, if he did not change. My father stopped drinking and stayed sober for the thirty-five years remaining in his life from that point. My mother's life was about the business of saving lives: as a nurse, as a wife, as a sister, and as a mother.

The last days of my mother's life were spent surrounded by family, friends, and the nuns of Saint Mary Star of the Sea on City Island. In her room at Calvary, she sat in the afternoons, when she was able, with my father reading the newspapers as they had always done at home, exchanging their identical views of the world that were identically shaped by the war in which they served. At night, she would hold her sickness in. On the several nights I spent there, she would wait until I awoke at her side, and she would say, "Get the bucket." I fumbled in the dark and, as always, stupidly, naively asking, "Why didn't you wake me?" But why didn't I just get the bucket quietly. Now I regret every hard word I ever spoke to her in my life. If only we could go back in time. If only I did not waste time with hard words. If only we could change the past and erase the mistakes.

My mother died in the morning hours of November 11, 2004, at Calvary Hospice on Eastchester Road in the Bronx. She died on Veterans Day, the same day, albeit a year later, at the same time of day, and of the same disease that killed her brother Matt.

On the day of her funeral, her coffin awaited entry to the church on the sidewalk leading to Saint Mary Star of the Sea on City Island. I watched her coffin from the church entry that was a few steps above the sidewalk as the United States Army covered her coffin with an American flag. Beyond the soldiers' slow, deliberate movements, the white caps of waves from the bay were quick and bright in the sun of a cold November day. My father stood facing her coffin. He was wearing a long gray wool coat and standing perfectly still as the US flag was laid precisely over her coffin. When the coffin was covered, my father slowly lifted his right hand and solemnly saluted his wife of sixty-four years. It was his final gift of abiding respect and rose forever above any other lesser moments from their lives.

I last saw my father at Christmas in 2012 when I visited City Island. He asked me to correct a war record. He told me about Bernie. He held his book of World War II warriors and pointed out that Bernie was not missing in action as was recorded in this book. He wanted me to write the army and correct the record. How could I do that? I did not know where to start.

Maybe I could find Bernie's family and tell them about Bernie's capture and probable murder by his Nazi captors. I wanted to try if that helped a personal history and if it would make my father feel better about the unfinished business of a war record he witnessed. When I returned home to North Carolina, I searched computer records but could find not a trace of the Berheim family from Berlin. This is how it was: the Nazis took Bernie and erased him without a trace or a record of what they had done. I realized then that every war would erase us but for the sacrifices of the many who run to the risk, to the fight, to the call, to the training, and to the war, including all the recruits and veterans I have written about here.

I tried to tell my father before he died that I was not going to be able to fix Bernie's record, but the last stages of congestive heart failure in 2013 were clouding his mind. I asked him if he received my letters that I sent in January of 2013, and he said he had not because he was traveling. He said that his father had come to travel with him. I asked, "Where are you traveling, Dad? Aren't you still on 25 Tier Street?"

He responded by asking, didn't I know that there were many places that are 25 Tier Street, his home, and that he was traveling to them with Poppy, his father. He said Poppy came to visit him every day, and Poppy looked great. Poppy looked better than him.

My father said he did not understand how it could be that Poppy, who was so much older than my father, looked better than he did. He asked Michael, his eldest son who once filled his earlier days with delightful stories from school, "How come Poppy looks so good? How come Poppy looks better than me?"

Michael told my father: "Poppy is dead, Dad; he has been dead for many years."

My father told me, "I am so grateful to have Michael to tell me these things."

I know, in the end, that it was Poppy who came for my father. My father did not take his final journey alone—none of us do. He, as my mother and as those who die believing in forgiveness, went straight up.

www.ingramcontent.com/pod-product-compliance
Lightning Source LLC
LaVergne TN
LVHW041315080426
835513LV00008B/473